ROTHERHAM UNITED

A PICTORIAL HISTORY

PAUL RICKETT

AMBERLEY

ACKNOWLEDGEMENTS

Thanks go to everyone who contributed to this book, either directly or indirectly, particularly the *Rotherham Advertiser* for the invaluable use of their archive material and images, stalwart historian Gerry Somerton, photographers Jim Brailsford and Paul Wickson, and everyone else who played their part.

Paul Rickett is the sports editor of the *Rotherham Advertiser* and has worked with the Millers for over twenty years. He was voted Yorkshire Sports Writer of the Year in 2008 and has been instrumental in other award-winning issues of the *Advertiser*, including a special Save the Millers magazine, published during the Millmoor financial crisis in 2007, given free of charge to the club and subsequently sold to raise funds. He has penned several other works on football and speedway racing.

First published 2013

Amberley Publishing
The Hill, Stroud
Gloucestershire, GL5 4EP

www.amberleybooks.com

Copyright © Paul Rickett, 2013

The right of Paul Rickett to be identified as the Author
of this work has been asserted in accordance with the
Copyrights, Designs and Patents Act 1988.

All rights reserved. No part of this book may be reprinted or reproduced or
utilised in any form or by any electronic, mechanical or other means, now known
or hereafter invented, including photocopying and recording, or in any information
storage or retrieval system, without the permission in writing from the Publishers.

British Library Cataloguing in Publication Data.
A catalogue record for this book is available from the British Library.

ISBN 978 1 4456 1358 1 (print)
ISBN 978 1 4456 1365 9 (ebook)

Typesetting and Origination by Amberley Publishing.
Printed in the UK.

IN THE BEGINNING

It was incredible to think that as Rotherham United ran out for their first-ever game at the plush, state-of-the-art New York Stadium in 2012, just a few soul-searching years earlier the club had been on the brink of shutting up shop for good.

Few people realise how serious the situation had become, as the Merry Millers teetered into the new century, exploded into the Championship, and then imploded dramatically, going within hours of having the padlocks snapped shut on the gates of their ramshackle Millmoor home.

Exactly how the club came through some turbulent and murky financial waters, right from day one of their existence, is one of football's success stories, amid what were some horrific boardroom decisions, the wielding of the longest of knives and even a splash of black magic. They may not have had a famous history, but Rotherham United certainly have a fascinating one.

Apocalyptic horizons have been commonplace since the foundations of the current club were laid late in the nineteenth century. Boardroom strife, as they say in deepest South Yorkshire, is nowt new.

There were plenty of teams playing in Rotherham in the formative years of the game; the first mention of a club in the town comes in 1867, with the rules for the town's inaugural team being formulated under the guidance of the town's enthusiastic Grammar School headmaster, the Revd J. J. Christie. The first recorded game in the town took place in December 1870, with a practice match between members of the new club at the Eastwood House ground on Doncaster Road. There were the romantically named Lunar Rovers, who played their games by moonlight at Clifton Grove – now a housing estate adjacent to the town's Herringthorpe fields – because the players couldn't get afternoons off work. The Rotherham Wanderers played at Jarvis' Field, which subsequently became the Clifton Lane ground, and several others sprang into life, such as Rotherham West End, Rotherham Swifts and Thornhill United, who kicked off their existence on 4 October 1877, at a pitch off Greasbrough Road near the town centre. Thornhill would go on to become a founding father of the current club.

Exactly when Rotherham United's roots were put down has always been a hot topic of debate amongst fans. Some say it has to be 1925, when the United name was first used; others believe it right to trace the club's family tree back to its origins. There is plenty of support for the latter argument. If United were borne out of an amalgamation between Rotherham County and Rotherham Town, then surely there is a case for plotting their formative clubs? County, for instance, stemmed from the Thornhill club, and its roots therefore go right back to 1877; Town evolved from the former Rotherham Club, which in turn was formerly the twilight-playing Lunar Rovers.

Confused? Even the historians were, when they decided for some reason that 1884 should be the official formation year, prior to launching the centenary celebrations in 1984. Maybe, for the sake of clarity, the club should bin the rest and stick to 1925.

Thornhill spent five years kicking about at Greasbrough Road before moving to the purpose-built, but nevertheless limited, Red House ground. It was spartan in the formative years, and wasn't much better by the time the club left in 1907. Red House was a hefty goal-kick away from Millmoor, and has long since disappeared, but originally it was situated on the New Wortley Road bypass next to Thornhill Primary School.

Thornhill played with a modicum of local success before changing their name to Rotherham County in 1905. They had generally played second fiddle to the town's other major team, Town.

Town had been eager to prove that they were the leading team in the borough when they entered all the leading cup competitions, but their first major hurdle was to find a suitable home after a falling-out with the Clifton Lane ground owners, who wanted a £5 rent increase. That saw Rotherham move down the road to a wholly unsuitable base at Wellgate, before switching to West End's former ground at Ickles. Eventually, they struck a new deal to move back to the Lane, with the promise of a new 500-seat stand being built, which was sited between the current cricket pavilion and scoreboard. That was when the name Town was officially adopted.

Success slowly came their way. Town first entered the English Cup in 1883/84, playing their maiden first-round tie on 10 November against Chesterfield side Spital. That ended 1-1, with Town winning the replay 7-2. In the second round, Town went down 3-1 at Sheffield Works side Lockwood Brothers.

Rotherham became founders of the Midland League in 1888, rubbing shoulders with the likes of The Wednesday and Preston North End, who won 3-1 at Clifton Lane that season in front of 4,000 fans. They beat Staveley at Bramall Lane to lift the Sheffield and Hallamshire Challenge Cup, earning an open-wagon parade through the town to mark their success.

In 1884, Rotherham were drawn at home to Nottingham Forest in the English Cup. The club played at the Clifton Lane sports ground, still in existence today as the home of Rotherham Titans Rugby Club, but accepted an offer of £17 10s to switch the tie to Forest's ground, where they were promptly thumped 5-0.

The following year, they were again drawn at home to the famous Notts County and this time sold their advantage for £30. The club went down 15-0 at Meadow Lane.

The passion for the game in the town was highlighted by an English Cup qualifying tie derby at Rotherham Swifts' ground across town at Holmes. The first game was abandoned for bad light, a commonplace occurrence in those days, which was also what happened at Clifton Lane as Town led 2-1 with six minutes to go. Swifts refused to concede. Town 'keeper Arthur Wharton – noted as the first black player in the English game – was kicked by an irate spectator and needed to go to hospital, while the unsporting Swifts team were pelted with mud and one of their players, Rab Howell, was hit with an umbrella!

But, in perhaps the first of several boardroom problems, Town again fell out of favour with the Clifton Lane authorities, and ended up moving to Lunar Rovers' old base at Clifton Grove at the end of the 1891 season, taking as many fixtures and fittings with them as they could. They kicked off at their new home when 3,000 supporters saw a 2-2 Midland League draw against Grantham.

After twice winning the Midland League, they were elected to the Football League's Second Division in 1893. The first League game in Rotherham took place on 9 September 1893, when Town beat Grimsby 4-3 in front of 2,500 fans – although the nerves on the opening day primarily stemmed from fears that a train full of Grimsby supporters could carry cholera into town, the disease having reached the port from the Continent. It didn't, but Rotherham nevertheless went on to suffer that year, claiming only five more victories to finish second from bottom of the table and having to apply for re-election.

Bootle and Northwich Victoria had both resigned from the League, leaving Rotherham and Manchester City to stand against prospective newcomers Leicester Fosse, Bury and Burton Wanderers. Rotherham garnered just fifteen votes to finish bottom of the pile, and looked to be heading back to the Midland League, until Middlesbrough Ironopolis also withdrew, saving the Clifton Grove side's bacon. Town were invited back in, but lasted only two more seasons. In 1895/96 they ended up twelfth and slumped back to second from bottom in the following campaign.

Biting finances – a local coal dispute having hit gate receipts – eventually proved fatal for the club, and in their last season an appeal for subscriptions from townsfolk brought in just enough money to prevent them from the ignominious fate of being the first Football League club to fold during a season. The last home game was a 2-2 draw against Lincoln City in front of a paltry 300 fans. Town didn't bother to apply for League status the following year and died away quietly, with Clifton Grove subsequently becoming a housing estate, which still stands today.

While Thornhill were plodding along in the Sheffield Association League, the embers of the old Town club had new life breathed into them two years later. In March 1898, a venture to relaunch the club fell flat, but in 1889 minor clubs Rotherham Casuals and the Grammar School merged to form Rotherham Club.

They joined the Sheffield Association alongside their rivals and became semi-pro at the turn of the century, playing back at Clifton Lane. They made efforts to make the ground more amenable for spectators, building banking and even buying the grandstand from the defunct racecourse at Herringthorpe. Club won the Sheffield Association Championship in 1903, Thornhill finishing runners-up, and both ambitious clubs switched to the Midland League, sparking a rivalry that was to last until their amalgamation in 1925.

Club revived the Rotherham Town name in 1905, a move that peeved Thornhill, who claimed they had more right to the town's name than their neighbours. So Thornhill became Rotherham County – named after the county borough – and with it came the decision to move grounds, especially when the ramshackle Red House was deemed unfit to stage English FA Cup ties. County agreed a deal to move to the Midland Railway-owned ground at Millmoor, a sloping plot of wasteland sandwiched between railway tracks and the tramlines stretching from Masbrough into town. An army of volunteers gave up their time to try and ease the slope, building terracing with ashes and railway sleepers, and even relocating two stands from Red House. Unlike the plush New York Stadium, Millmoor was far lower key. The two Red House stands were pieced together to form one on the Millmoor Lane side, and to stop people from having a free view from the main roadway, a huge 30-foot hoarding was erected.

In a sweet twist of irony, prior to the enclosure-side main stand being erected, new changing rooms and offices were built with bricks donated from the Midland Iron Co., while the windows and doors were sourced from an old cottage property sited where the New York Stadium now proudly sits. What few fans know is that the ground was originally to be called the Coronation Ground, a name that was subsequently dropped. By the time the work had finished, Millmoor could accommodate 15,000 spectators and, more importantly, was given the thumbs-up by the FA.

The first game at the new ground was on 2 September 1907, when County beat Leeds City Reserves in the Midland League, Algernon Pynegar having the honour of scoring the first goal. In the build-up to the First World War, County became the dominant club, winning four successive Midland League titles, and they were invited to join the new Second Division of the Football League in 1919. In their maiden campaign they finished seventeenth in the new tier, including a new best of 18,000 spectators watching a 1-1 draw with eventual champions Tottenham Hotspur.

The following year a new stand was erected at Millmoor, the crowd record was increased to 21,000 for the derby win over Sheffield Wednesday, and Rotherham went on to finish nineteenth. Their tenure in Division Two was to last two more years, with sixteenth place in 1921/22 and then a disastrous campaign that saw then end second from the bottom. Not only were County hit with a fine for making illegal payments to an amateur – the player, G. W. Cook, had his registration cancelled and four officials were suspended for a year – but the biggest downer came with the club's relegation to the new Third Division North.

County did pull their socks up, finishing fourth in their debut season in the Third Division, and there were high hopes of promotion the next time around. That never materialised and County had a dreadful year, finishing eleven points adrift at the bottom – the only time a Rotherham team finished bottom of the pile in the Football League. It was clear that changes needed to be made.

The only bright spot that year came in the final weeks of County's existence. The Sheffield and Hallamshire County Cup semi-final was played at Millmoor, with FA Cup winners Sheffield United the visitors. The Bramall Lane club fielded the side that had beaten Cardiff City at Wembley, and paraded the trophy through Rotherham prior to the game. County promptly went out and, despite their position at the foot of the League, beat United 4-1, with Harold Hamilton hitting a hat-trick. It was described in the *Advertiser* as 'one of the greatest triumphs in County's history' and made some amends for the club's perilous position.

But if County were struggling, it was a catastrophic time over at Town. They had hoped to be admitted to the new Third Division and plans to develop Clifton Lane were put in place. But the ambitious Midland League clubs, who were eyeing a move up, were put in an impossible situation. Resignations had to be submitted by 1 March 1921, prior to the date of the Football League's formation of the new Northern section. Confidently, Town slapped in their resignation, only to receive just thirteen votes and be told they wouldn't be accepted into the League.

It was clear that Rotherham just couldn't support two major clubs; attendances were falling at both grounds and there were hints of an amalgamation in 1922. Representatives of the FA and Football League were present at meetings of the shareholders of both Town and County when it was said in no uncertain terms that one of the two would have to go. It was a case of the survival of the fittest and Town were the ones to fall.

They found it increasingly difficult to make ends meet and, after a torrid 1922 season, when they finished second from the bottom, the following year they dropped to the bottom. By then any hopes of following County into the League were straight out of the window and amalgamation talks gathered momentum, with crowds so poor that players were asked to take a cut in wages – something that would reoccur eighty-five years later – and were give the option to move on if they wished.

The outlook was bleak for both clubs and finally the link-up was agreed on Saturday 28 February 1925. Local newspaper the *Advertiser* commented:

> We have now entered upon what is virtually the last month of the present football season – a season that has been the most distressing in the history of Rotherham football since the fateful one in 1895/96 when the old Town club, finding itself unable to continue its association with the Football League, simply dropped out of it and, by going into voluntary liquidation, just ceased to exist.
>
> A long and pathetic story could be written of the old and original Town club, an organisation that was victim to untoward circumstances, the chief of which was a ruinous coal strike that crippled the club's finances.
>
> Exactly thirty years have elapsed since the original Town club had to cry 'enough!' Rotherham has changed in many ways since then.
>
> Our duty at this time is to avoid a repetition of that tragedy and it can only be avoided everybody putting his and her heart into the work which has to be done. For the past three seasons, football in Rotherham has been descending. It has now dropped to its lowest level and it has got to be helped up the hill.

And so with the birth of Rotherham United, which was officially ratified on 27 May 1925, came the fresh hope of a new dawn.

But more footballing catastrophes were lurking on the horizon.

Rotherham Town in 1892.

Thornhill United in 1893/94 with the Rotherham Charity Cup.

Rotherham Town in 1901.

Workmen at Millmoor in 1907.

Inset: Rotherham County logo.

Above: Rotherham County, 1911.

Below: Rotherham County, 1912.

2

AN UNHAPPY MARRIAGE

Rotherham United got off to an inauspicious start when they played their first game, despite all the optimism that came with the new club.

It had been decided to clear the boards completely. 'These are momentous days for Rotherham football,' said the club. 'They are days of change and from the process of transition, there is to emerge the Rotherham United club – an organisation with a new name, a strong and virile body and with a determination to realise ambitions.'

Out went the previous black-and-white striped shirts of the County club, and the chocolate-and-light-blue and then blue-and-white of Town. In came a new amber shirt with a black V across the chest, and they brought in several new players.

But they certainly came home from the Division Three (North) opener at Bradford on 29 August with their tails between their legs. Clearly outplayed, they were hammered 6-1, with Jack Hammerton having the distinction of scoring the club's first-ever goal. Nearly 6,000 fans watched the first home game two days later, when Tranmere Rovers were beaten 2-0, and that initial optimism really was rekindled when they then beat Grimsby Town. In what was to become typical Rotherham United style, the highs were quickly followed by the lows.

They signed forward Ernest Goldthorpe from Manchester United, but his contract was cancelled after just two games when he suffered a leg injury. His last game was a 3-1 reverse against Nelson when the referee reported sections of the Millmoor crowd for bad behaviour, with warning notices being posted around the ground.

United beat First Division Bury in the FA Cup, a record 16,442 seeing a gallant display in the club's first-ever third-round game before United went down 3-2. That put much needed cash in the coffers. After all, the amalgamation scheme had been costly and the trend of financial hardship hadn't been swept away by the new broom. Indeed, there were major worries within the boardroom – so much so that it was feared the club could break up.

United lost nearly £2,000 in their first season, despite salaries having been cut from the previous year, and crowds hadn't responded in the way it had been hoped. All of the playing squad were made available for transfer.

One concern, something that irks present-day Millers fans, was the number of people who travelled to Sheffield to watch their football. While Rotherham were struggling with crowds – the average attendance was 5,384 and the numbers tailed off alarmingly towards the end, with just 1,928 watching the season-ending 2-2 draw with Crewe – thousands were seen flocking to Bramall Lane and Hillsborough. Over 4,000 people from town packed the trams and buses for the Blades' game against Huddersfield, and twice that number were believed to have watched the FA Cup fourth-round tie between Sheffield United and Sunderland on the same afternoon that Rotherham drew 5,300 for their League game against Halifax! In the end, Rotherham finished fourteenth in their maiden campaign, enough to offer optimism on the field for the following year.

The club cut their season ticket prices to try and increase the turnstile clicks, and they even signed high-profile Northern Ireland international Harry Pantling from the Blades. They started well enough, with wins over Crewe and Wrexham, but the 1926/27 season mirrored the previous one. Rotherham again struggled to attract the support they needed, and the fallout from the General Strike of that summer didn't help. Mineworkers remained embroiled in industrial disputes long after the strike ended and that certainly impacted on crowds. The biggest queues at the ground were outside the boys' gate, despite many being well over-age, and the club made moves to stop the practice.

The good start tailed off. United struggled to win and slipped down the table. Pantling was released and joined non-League Heanor; Beighton-born Jackie Bestall, a star of the previous campaign, was sold to Grimsby; and hopes that a good cup run might raise enthusiasm came to an abrupt halt with a 2-0 defeat at Lincoln City. They finished nineteenth that year, breathing a sigh of relief that they didn't have to apply for re-election. With the financial troubles continuing, that might just have seen United disappear out of the League.

The next eleven seasons leading up to the Second World War saw much of the same. The 1927/28 campaign started badly with a 2-0 defeat at Stockport. It was the start of eight miserable away games that brought just one point, before a morale-boosting 5-2 Christmas victory at Chesterfield, twenty-four hours after a 2-1 Boxing Day defeat at Millmoor. Rotherham's home form was much better, and that helped keep them away from the potential trapdoor at the bottom.

The highlights of that year were home wins over neighbours Doncaster Rovers, a 2-1 victory in February in front of 11,530, and a 1-0 win against eventual champions Bradford Park Avenue.

One big cloud over the club came with the death of seventy-one-year-old Bill Wordsworth, the chairman who had helped steer Rotherham through some stormy waters.

They wrapped up the year in fourteenth, and in 1928/29 it was another struggle, although having only made a loss of £30 there was optimism that they could be turning the corner. It was also notable in that United decided to ditch their amber-and-black kit and change to red shirts, white shorts and black socks with a red-and-white top – the directors hoping that changing to brighter colours would improve their luck. The squad was also revamped and United promptly ran out for their opener at Bradford City and ran back in with their tails 'twixt their legs after an 11-1 thumping. Later in the year, they were also battered 10-1 at South Shields, the only season when they twice conceded double-figure scores.

But as in previous seasons, it was the home form that kept them out of danger, with twelve wins. Yet crowds continued to dwindle on the back of the win-some, lose-some results. At the turn of the roaring twenties, attendances of over 10,000 were commonplace, with the record having been 21,000 against Sheffield Wednesday in November 1920. Three years into the new era, average gates were down to 4,529. They again dwindled alarmingly towards the end when Rotherham finished sixteenth – doubtless spectators were getting fed up of more of the same each year – and not one attendance hit double figures.

It did get worse. But in 1929/30, Rotherham had taken the bold step of appointing Welsh international Stan Davies as player-manager. Stan, formerly of Everton, Preston, West Bromwich Albion, Cardiff and Birmingham, had taken charge prior to the final game of the previous year and made an immediate impact as his side beat Rochdale 5-0. That, plus the recruitment of several new players, sent hopes soaring.

Davies was a major signing. Capped eighteen times for his country, his playing career was ebbing to an end and he played only five times for United, only one of those coming in the League. He was Rotherham's first real 'manager' in that beforehand the directors had the main say on all matters, including team selection, but now Davies was given a free hand.

Yet, once again, they made another inconsistent start, twice conceding five goals in their opening three away games, losing 5-4 at Halifax in the curtain-raiser and crashing 5-1 at Barrow. Rotherham won only three games in their opening thirteen and, just as it looked as though the tide was being turned with a 2-1 victory over Crewe, Davies' side promptly lost 7-1 at Southport.

Fans never knew what to expect that season. One minute they were thumping Tranmere 5-0 at Millmoor, and then being battered 5-1 at Hartlepool next time out. They battered Barrow 7-0, Egbert Murden hitting four goals in the way to a season tally of twenty-two; the first United player to breach the twenty-goal mark, and the first to do so for the club since Jack Hammerton's twenty-four for County eight years earlier. That win was followed by a string of horrendous results heading into the New Year: they lost 4-0 at home to Rochdale, 5-0 at South Shields, 4-2 against Accrington at Millmoor and then 8-1 and 7-1 at Darlington and Port Vale respectively.

If ever there was a season of roller-coaster results, this was it. The grim run ended with a 4-1 victory over Wigan Borough in front of just 1,600 fans – who by this time were voting with their feet – only to go on and lose 6-1 at Stockport, 5-2 at home to York and 6-1 at Crewe in consecutive outings. On the flip side, Rotherham did beat Southport 6-3 and walloped Carlisle 4-1, only for the campaign to end with a 4-0 drubbing at home to Hartlepool.

The season couldn't end quickly enough. Davies was the subject of abuse from the crowd and even wrote to the *Advertiser* saying he'd never kick a ball for the club again. He eventually resigned in March 1930.

3

MORE DIFFICULT TIMES

The fusion of football in the town hadn't worked.

Yes, the two ailing clubs had merged to form the new club, and despite all the monetary struggles, not helped by ongoing industrial problems in the region, at least there was still a team in Rotherham. Yet United had found it very tough going on and off the field, and the bright new dawn simply didn't materialise in the way it was hoped. That was to continue into the thirties, as the club continued to teeter from one financial crisis to another.

It kicked off in the very first year of the decade; renewed optimism on the terraces – or old railway sleepers as they were in those days – fell flat when an appeal was launched in the summer of 1930 for investment. The mayor, Alderman E. Cruikshank, led the campaign and he headed a committee trying to raise £2,000 for the club (almost £100,000 in today's money).

United continued to lose cash – just £864 compared to the £1,952 from the previous year – but they nevertheless invested in the side by bringing in Billy Hick from Notts County and goalkeeper James Harris from Manchester City. Hick had been around the block before coming to Millmoor, playing for a string of lower league clubs, and he was an instant success. He was signed in mid-September, by which time Rotherham had got off to another inconsistent start, with three unbeaten games for starters being followed by three defeats.

Hick's first game was against Barrow at home and he promptly whacked a hat-trick in a 6-0 win. Rotherham then went to Southport and lost 4-1, before Accrington came to town and Hick walloped another three in an 8-1 thumping – only for the club to crash 6-1 at Rochdale seven days later. Hick scored the consolation in that one, and went on to bag thirty goals in thirty-one appearances during the campaign, the first Rotherham player to do so. He went on to score five hat-tricks that year.

Fans thought United were onto a winner, especially with forward partner Vic Wright also scoring regularly. He scored eight in the opening seven games, including four in the win over Accrington, but the two were split up when Wright moved on to Sheffield Wednesday for an undisclosed but still club record fee.

But perhaps the most important signing came that season. Defender Reg Freeman arrived at Millmoor after spending seven years with Middlesbrough, and before that started his professional career with Oldham. An accomplished full-back, Freeman made thirty appearances in his maiden year, but he'd be remembered later as the man who helped steer the club out of the doldrums.

Conceding seventeen goals in four games in December set the hallmark for the rest of the programme, and Rotherham slipped to fourteenth place in the final reckonings.

There was little to enthuse about in the cup either. The year before, Rotherham had reached the third round before losing at Nottingham Forest. This time they were embarrassingly ousted 2-1 by minnows Newark Town of the Midland League.

But 1930/31 was notable on another tack. It was the year that the club's now familiar nickname was born. Thought to derive from the fact that two windmills once stood on the town centre landscape, the new Supporters' Club originally opted for the nickname for themselves but it quickly stuck with the team ... and so the Merry Millers were born.

It was increasingly obvious, throughout the game, that new revenue streams were needed and the board hit upon the idea of introducing greyhound racing at Millmoor. A track was constructed for the summer months and the venture was an immediate success, the first meeting taking place on Monday 11 May 1931. It was to last for two years.

Meanwhile, a raft of new signings perked up interest in 1931/32, but it quickly became evident that United couldn't shrug off their bad old ways. Fans never knew what to expect as the team had convincing early home wins over Rochdale and Doncaster, winning 5-1 and 6-3 respectively, sandwiched either side of a 6-1 drubbing at Tranmere.

Just three wins from the first three games saw Rotherham slide down the table and attendances also dropped alarmingly. Billy Hick's goals also dried up, and he was dropped after a Boxing Day defeat at home to Crewe, never to play again.

Supporters certainly voted with their feet in those days. The opening crowd of 6,431 for the beating of Rochdale was countered by just 2,240 turning up to watch a December draw with New Brighton. Receipts simply weren't enough to pay the bills, and fears began to resurface that the club would keel over under the weight of mounting debt. Before the end of the season, the directors again issued a plea for help, underlined by the end-of-season accounts, which showed an annual loss of £2,155. That took the club's total liability to a whopping £14,230 – over £700,000 in today's terms – and they appealed to supporters who still owed season ticket money from the start of the season to pay up.

On the park, the gloom was mirrored by a final finish in nineteenth place. It was only a flourish in their final few games – seven wins from ten games – that spared the ignominy of having to apply for re-election.

The next campaign was more of the same. Wages had been trimmed to a minimum. Topsy-turvy results included a 9-2 Christmas beating at Mansfield, which came just twenty-four hours after the Stags had been beaten 3-0 at Millmoor on Boxing Day. They also suffered an 8-0 defeat at Crewe, but the fans' ire was tempered by a 6-1 thrashing of Halifax in the finale, played out in front of a mere 1,588. That season was also the first time the Merry Millers had failed to win an away match, taking just three draws from twenty-one outings. No surprise, then, that United failed to get above halfway and finished seventeenth.

By 1933/34, Rotherham's directors must have thought they'd killed a tramcar full of black cats. Little did they know that they were about to make one of the best moves in the club's history.

At the time, they were despondent to find out from the Football Association that greyhound racing should no longer take place at the grounds. As United had tapped into a vital revenue stream despite the fact that players often complained because the edges of the pitch were churned up where the track was laid, the FA instructed that football should not be supported – or even controlled – by greyhounds. This didn't go down too well at Millmoor, considering the board had just signed another twelve-month lease with the racing company. The final dogs meeting was on 29 July 1933, and that meant the club was forced to implement more strict cash-saving measures. That, of course, meant a cut in quality on the pitch and the Merry Millers were beaten six times in their first seven games, a 5-1 battering at Chester on opening day setting the tone for a miserable season.

The tide was stemmed as local lad Richard Sykes was switched from outside-left to centre-half to shore up the defence, and Rotherham managed to avoid any more heavy defeats, although they couldn't avoid slumping to second from bottom and had to endure the worry of re-election, having finished above Rochdale but five points adrift of Accrington.

Crowd levels were also a major issue. The disappointing end to a disappointing season – the worst since County finished bottom the season before amalgamation – saw a succession of sub-3,000 attendances, with a new low of just 1,324 watching a 2-1 home defeat against neighbours Mansfield on the final Saturday.

But 1933/34 hadn't all been gloom and despondency. United had a good run in the FA Cup before losing in front of 20,000 fans to Wednesday at Hillsborough in the third round. And perhaps the major event of the year came with the appointment of Reg Freeman as manager in January. Ironically, he played his final game on New Year's Day in a 5-1 thrashing at rivals Barnsley and, after hanging up his boots, took charge in time for the Wednesday Cup tie, which Rotherham lost 3-0. Little did anyone realise at the time, but Freeman would go on to become one of the most revered of United's managers.

The directors had realised that they needed someone at the helm, rather than being in charge of team matters themselves. It simply wasn't working. Freeman was to stabilise the club and turn it into a force following the war years. His first managerial wrinkles probably appeared during the close season as Rotherham waited to learn their fate following the nervous re-election process. Thankfully, only Nelson applied – unsuccessfully – and both Rotherham and Rochdale were left to fight another day. Initially, Freeman found it tough going but, despite a career as a defender, stuck to his principles of attacking football. He brought in new players and there was fresh optimism around the club. From the miserable attendance that saw the final game of the 1933/34 season, over 8,000 turned up to watch the opening-day draw with Chesterfield and over 7,000 saw another 2-2 scoreline against Chester two days later.

But the results didn't come and, just as brows were again beginning to furrow, new signing Roland Bastow went on to net eighteen goals, forming a strong partnership up front with Billy Dickinson, who had been brought in from Nottingham Forest during the summer and was ever-present, scoring twenty-five times. But despite the increasing stability on the pitch, there were more worries off it.

Since Millmoor had been opened, it had been owned and leased by the LMS Railway Company and, in December 1934, they decided to offer the freehold of the site by auction.

Even though it was initially offered at £3,000, for some reason the LMS withdrew the lot when the bidding had reached £4,800. They then announced that the rental agreement with the club, due to expire the following May, was to be increased three-fold and renegotiated on an annual basis, and United went cap-in-hand to the borough council in an appeal for help.

The club's reaction was to look for an alternative site. Clifton Lane was off the agenda, so attention switched to an empty tract of land on Eldon Road – which is still being used for local football to this day. It was hemmed in by housing development, but the club began to think positively about building a new 30,000-capacity ground, and the council went as far as to offer them initial rental terms of £50 per annum.

Whether it was a case of brinkmanship or whether the railway company bowed to public opinion, the terms offered on Millmoor were amended to include a reduction in the rental demand and a longer lease. United accepted, and Freeman and his team were able to get on with the job of challenging in the rarefied air of the top half of the division. A string of good results even brought whispers of possible promotion, unheard of in Rotherham, but they eventually finished ten points off second-placed Halifax in a very respectable ninth.

Billy Dickinson was again at it in 1935/36, scoring a whirlwind nine goals in the first six games with Bastow again an able foil. The Merry Millers had brought in eleven new players, the ground had been smartened up and even a new gym had been built beneath the main stand, but despite Dickinson's heroics Rotherham again flattered to deceive, and started with three straight defeats.

Freeman stuck to his guns, and the turn-around came with a 5-0 victory against Southport, Rotherham losing just one of their next eleven. They finished eleventh that year, again with the win-some, lose-some culture that had dominated their first ten years since amalgamation.

Dickinson moved on just before the end of the season, sold to Southend United, with Ernest Smith, signed the previous year from Nottingham Forest, taking over the mantle up front for 1936/37. Smith linked well with Bastow, the two scoring twenty-two and twelve goals respectively, while left-winger Ralph Pedwell also grabbed the headlines with twenty. This time around, the terrace groaners were given plenty of fodder as United shipped a mini-avalanche of goals at the start of 1937, not winning in twelve and slumping to the bottom of the table.

Freeman kept confidence in the side, refused to panic, and a 3-1 triumph over Tranmere on 20 March – their first victory of the year – eased the plight. Rotherham went on to win five of their final seven matches to end up in seventeenth.

On the financial front, there was still some nervous thumbing of the accounts ledger. Outgoing transfers meant the club showed a slight profit, although an overall debt of £12,400 meant Freeman's hands were tied as far as signing players, and the emphasis was placed on developing young talent. When Rotherham won their opening two games of 1937/38 it set the agenda for the club's best season yet. Forward Arnold Bramham, born in West Melton but who had started his career with Notts County, had an innocuous first season at Millmoor the year before but shot to prominence with twenty-two goals, making up for the previously prolific Ernest Smith's lack of goals – a modest ten – despite having played in every game. They were dogged by injury but results continued to go their way and six wins in seven games brought about a massive first for the club – the first time any Rotherham team had topped their division.

A 2-0 victory at Tranmere on New Year's Day sent promotion hopes soaring and, for the first time, fans were able to feel good about the club and its prospects. But when they lost 3-1 at Oldham a week later they were deposed and slid down to fourth. United did nose back up to joint top, but a run of mixed results saw them drop down the table as Freeman juggled with his team permutations due to injuries. Still, Rotherham were pleased to finish a best-ever sixth as United, just four points away from a promotion place.

Three straight wins at the beginning of 1938/39 propelled United to the top of the early rankings, thanks to an opening day 7-1 blasting of Rochdale, with Bramham scoring four, while the striker then netted a brace in a 4-1 victory at Crewe two days later. When the Merry Millers won 1-0 at York the following week, optimism abounded. They had a hiccup in the shape of a 2-0 setback at Barnsley, but then eased home 3-0 against Wrexham before Barnsley came to town and did the double with a solitary goal victory. Nevertheless, crowds of 10,419 and a hefty 20,144 for the latter two respectively underlined the fact that the supporters had plenty of faith that United could kick on and better the previous season.

But the old gremlin continued to affect them. In successive games, they were hammered 7-1 at Gateshead, thrashed Hartlepool's 5-1, lost 3-1 at Darlington and beat Carlisle 4-0 before going on a four-game losing streak that saw the side slide down the table. If you wanted inconsistency, Rotherham was the club to follow.

They took seven games in the New Year before recording a win, and uncertainty over the future of Reg Freeman seemed to hamper the team. Freeman had been made a tempting offer to take over at fellow Division Three (North) side Stockport but, to everyone's relief at Millmoor, chose to stay. Rotherham ended a relatively disappointing eleventh – only a handful of years earlier they'd have happily settled for that – and the old financial worries resurfaced when chairman Edgar Jenkins announced that the club needed to increase income after struggling to survive ever since the amalgamation. They were only spared more losses after selling several players and bringing in £2,600 in transfer fees. But all that was overshadowed as the clouds of war began to loom.

Rotherham, as with every other club, began preparations for the 1939/40 season despite the growing uncertainty in Europe. Mark Hooper, a legend down the road after scoring 125 goals in 384 games for Wednesday, was signed and was expected to pass on vital experience to the younger players as player-coach.

But it wasn't to be. Rotherham did kick off the season with a 3-1 defeat at Tranmere and then beat York 2-1 at Millmoor before drawing 2-2 with Darlington. But when war was declared on 3 September, the government called a halt to all sports until further notice.

Rotherham's revival had been halted by a certain Adolf Hitler.

The state-of-the-art Millmoor Lane stand being built in 1928.

Rotherham United, 1931.

Above: How
Millmoor looked
from the air in 1935.

Left: Rotherham
United, 1936.

4

OH, WHAT A LOVELY WAR

Football was, of course, put on hold by the Second World War. With the Football League suspended, eleven days after the outbreak of hostilities it was announced that competitions would be resumed with strict limitations, and ten regional wartime divisions were devised, although not to form part of any official records. That was especially so because so many players left to join the Army and clubs were allowed to use guests. Rotherham, for example, used Sheffield United star Harold Barton during their North Regional League campaign in 1944/45, but Barton also represented Wednesday, Bradford, Chesterfield and Lincoln City during the seven wartime seasons. Jackie Stamps, who went on to legendary status with Derby County, also turned out in the red-and-white.

Travel was limited to a 50-mile radius and crowd limits of 8,000 were initially imposed. Rotherham joined the East Midlands League, and won seven of their twenty games, the worst result being a 6-1 defeat at Chesterfield, who went on to win the title. In the War Cup, the Merry Millers bowed out after a 3-0 second-round replay defeat at home to Sheffield United.

The following seasons they joined the North Regional League. In 1940/41, United won twelve of their twenty-eight games but bowed out of the War Cup, again losing 3-0 at home to the Blades. In 1941/42, Rotherham won only six of their eighteen matches, again losing out to Sheffield United in the War Cup. But that was the season that Walter Ardron arrived on the scene at Millmoor, having signed for £750 from local club Denaby United in December 1938.

Ardron had played as a twenty-year-old in the final year of League competition, making one appearance on 14 January in a forgettable 2-0 defeat at Wrexham. He played the first two years of the war at Derby but then returned to his home-town club and just couldn't stop scoring. He netted five goals in four consecutive games at the end of the season and also hit nine in six games in the War Cup as Rotherham were again beaten by the Blades.

It was the start of an astonishing career at Millmoor for Swinton-born Wally. He smashed 123 goals in five wartime seasons, which culminated in United's first-ever trophy success. That came in 1945/46, and victory in the war saw the move back towards proper competition with the formation of the Third Division (East), and United winning twelve of their eighteen games. The War Cup was consigned to history and the FA Cup reintroduced, being staged over two legs for the first time, and Rotherham going out on aggregate to Barnsley.

But it was the Third Division Cup that brought the first-ever silverware to the club. They progressed through the qualifying stage to reach the two-leg knockout rounds. United beat Wrexham, Doncaster and Gateshead to go through to the final, where they met Chester. By then, another new face was starting to emerge. Doncaster-born Jack Shaw was brought into the side and netted six times, including a brace in the 2-2 first-leg draw and the winner in the 3-2 second leg at Sealand Road, with Burke and Dawson adding the others.

Everything looked rosy in the Millmoor garden heading into the resumption of League fixtures in 1946/47 – but before the club embarked on what would be their most successful era in modern football, there was the little matter of hanging on to the prolific Wally Ardron.

The prolific Wally Ardron in action at Millmoor.

5

ARDRON SPARKS
SOMETHING SPECIAL

Wally Ardron had been a revelation since joining the Millers from minnows Denaby, but his wartime exploits hadn't gone unnoticed. When contracts were offered prior to the 1946/47 resumption, Ardron said he wanted better than Third Division football. But Rotherham didn't want to let him go, and contacted both the Football League and FA for advice. They said that without the club's consent he wouldn't be allowed to move anywhere.

United blocked his path out of Millmoor and, after the two parties held talks, Ardron shook hands with manager Reg Freeman and embarked on an astounding three years, before he was finally tempted away after scoring 102 goals in three unmatched seasons. He banged home forty goals in his first full season and what was to be a memorable period at the club.

It was the start of United's golden decade, Freeman having brought in the likes of Jack Shaw, who would also go on to be one of Rotherham's most prolific marksmen, Barnsley-born Stewart McLean, and a certain Gladstone Guest, who eventually became holder of the club's League scoring record. Freeman also signed Rotherham youngsters Danny Williams and his namesake, Horace – although no relation – while local lad Albert Wilson was signed from Crystal Palace.

It was the start of something special. Freeman's side oozed potential and quality, and hopes that this Rotherham team would surpass any other – not difficult really, considering the seemingly continual battle simply to survive – would quickly be realised.

United started like a train. They went to Tranmere and won 4-1 with Ardron, Wilson, McLean and Guest on the scoresheet, setting the hallmark for the year as those four ended up as the top-scoring quartet with a thundering ninety-one goals between them. Rotherham won at York two days later and in their home opener, post-war enthusiasm on the terraces saw nearly 15,000 turn up for a 4-1 demolition of Darlington. Wins followed at Hull and against Gateshead – a 4-0 romp – and then a 5-1 thrashing of Crewe in which Ardron netted four goals.

Despite a 4-0 setback at Lincoln, Rotherham then went on an eleven-match unbeaten run, winning eight, which included a 1-1 draw against Doncaster at Belle Vue. Both sides were piling on the points and it was the first salvo in a rivalry that saw both sides fighting it out for the one promotion place.

The crowds certainly rallied to the cause, and the club didn't see a gate of below 10,000 prior to Christmas, with a capacity 18,000 watching a 3-1 Boxing Day win over Chester – Ardron scoring the lot. Two days later, United battered Tranmere in front of 16,000 and then crushed York City 6-1 on New Year's Day. Fifteen goals in the space of a week – no wonder the supporters were in ferment.

It didn't stop there, with the Millers sweeping all before them at home. Two weeks after the York goal frenzy they demolished Halifax 6-1 and the goals continued to flow, topping off with an 8-0 beating of Oldham in May, as Ardron scored his second hat-trick in a fortnight after again hitting the lot in the earlier 3-0 win over Lincoln.

They remained unbeaten at home all season, but on the flip side, Rotherham's away form let them down, as the seven defeats gave Doncaster the upper hand in the title race. The two met for the second time at Millmoor on 26 April, when a season high of 20,237 saw United win 3-2 thanks to Len Hainsworth, McLean and Shaw. But the win wasn't enough to topple Rovers from top spot, as they took the title by eight points and United had to settle for the runners-up spot.

They also missed out on what would have been the incredible feat of winning all their home games. United needed to beat Rochdale at Millmoor to go through the card. They drew 3-3 after Dale survived a frenzied last twenty minutes in which the Millers threw everything bar the dressing room furniture at them.

It was a season of other firsts, with Ardron's new goals record, and the biggest crowd they'd ever played in front of (43,119) in a battling 3-0 FA Cup defeat at mighty Wolves – a little-known fact that's unlikely ever to be surpassed. That's because in 1946/47, *every* League goal was scored by a locally born player. Ardron hit thirty-eight; Wilson and McLean added nineteen each; Guest netted fifteen; Shaw scored thirteen times; and the others came from Hainsworth (6), Jack Edwards (1), Joe Dawson (1) and Danny Williams (1). All were from Rotherham apart from Sheffielder Dawson and Doncaster-born Shaw – but they were both club products. The board had wanted Reg Freeman to develop his own talent and he certainly did that.

It certainly wasn't a disappointment to finish second, and hopes soared for the following campaign, with the enterprising United side producing so many goals.

Speedy winger Albert Wilson moved on to Grimsby, but he would be back at Millmoor in later years as groundsman, while Ardron agreed terms for another season, despite more worries that he'd be on the move. Understandably, the stunning goals record from the entire strike force the previous year had scouts flocking to the ground, and Freeman had the unenviable job of trying to keep as many of his players as he could. Several were still part-timers, working at the pit or steelworks, and training was still held on a piece of wasteland near the ground, so no wonder the bright lights proved tempting. Can you imagine any of today's players heading off to a night shift after playing a game? It happened in those days.

Over 12,000 watched the first game, a 0-0 draw with Gateshead, before United cranked up the enthusiasm by heading to Oldham and winning 5-1. It was the start of another exemplary year at home, which brought some punishing wins. They blasted Carlisle 7-2, Wrexham and New Brighton 6-0, Carlisle 5-1 and Oldham, Bradford, Rochdale and Stockport 4-1. Ardron again couldn't stop scoring, netting four against Carlisle to celebrate the birth of his son, and even though his forward partners didn't show the support of previous years – Guest, Shaw and newcomer Ronnie Thompson, signed from Wednesday, each scoring ten – United still pushed for the top.

It was the six-goal thrashing of Wrexham that really sent pulses racing. The Welshmen had been a point clear of the Millers at the top before that beating, which saw Freeman's side go top for the first time. They flirted with the top spot into the New Year and beyond, and went on a stunning run of nine wins from ten, which saw them ideally placed for the run-in.

After thirty-six matches, they were level at the top on fifty-one points with Lincoln City. Rotherham then went to lowly Rochdale and lost 1-0, sparking anger from the travelling fans that accused the board of not wanting the team to go up. That became a common cry over the years, albeit without any justification.

It set the scene for one of Rotherham's biggest showdowns to date. Lincoln came to town on 24 April in the penultimate game of the season, with United knowing that a win would be enough to take them up. Over 20,000 packed into Millmoor for the game, but two goals in the opening ten minutes – the only two of the game – meant that City went top and everything rested on the final day. Rotherham went to Accrington's Peel Park and won 1-0, thanks to an Ardron goal, but the army of followers were disappointed when news filtered through that Lincoln had beaten Hartlepool 5-0.

So it was another frustrating end to a season that had promised so much – and United's burgeoning golden generation would have to endure more of the same in 1948/49.

That summer saw Rotherham invited to play in a tournament in Holland, including a 4-0 victory over Ajax, while off the field the big news was that the club purchased Millmoor from the LSM Railway Company on 7 May for £5,500 (£135,000 in today's money) and plans were immediately put in place to develop the ground. The club had even made a hefty profit the previous season, thanks to an average home attendance of 14,000 and every crowd being over 10,000. Ardron agreed to stay at the club and continue the prolific partnership with Guest and Shaw, while another youth protégé, Barnsley-born Jack Grainger, became established on the wing after making a handful of appearances the year before. Grainger went on to become the darling of the terraces and played at Rotherham for eleven seasons, making over 300 appearances, before joining Lincoln after a terrific record that saw him score more than a goal a game. Grainger was able to provide another attacking dimension while Freeman moved to bring in Colin Rawson from Peterborough and also Norman Noble from Bradford City. Noble, also Barnsley-born, went on to be another stalwart servant, remembered – wrongly – for a certain day at Port Vale in 1955 ... But more of that later.

The Millers kicked off in 1948 with a sensational run of ten wins in eleven games, including a 7-0 blitz against Tranmere and a 4-0 victory at Wrexham. They also won 4-1 at Hartlepool with Ardron celebrating his son's first birthday by repeating his feat in the week the lad was born – hitting four goals! The run ended with a 2-0 defeat at fellow promotion challengers Darlington, but United promptly went out and won their next five, culminating in a 6-1 thrashing of Crewe – Ardron hitting a hat-trick.

Unbelievably, the bubble seemed to have burst when they lost 6-1 at York. But any moans and groans were silenced as Rotherham caned Carlisle 8-1 next time out. Tom

Lowder, from Worksop but who had been playing as an amateur at Crystal Palace, banged a hat-trick on his debut, and Ardron wasn't to be outdone as he also netted three. It was the last of his record nine hat-tricks for the Millers.

But while Rotherham had been flying, Yorkshire rivals Hull City were also doing very nicely at their new Boothferry Park ground. By Christmas it was clear that the two sides would slug it out for the promotion place. The key fixtures came on Christmas Day, when United lost 3-2 at Boothferry in front of a massive crowd of 54,652, and the following afternoon the sides met against at Millmoor and 22,159 saw a 0-0 draw. Rotherham went into the year three points ahead of City but ominously having played two games more.

Around Easter, they went on another long, unbeaten run, this time ten games, and it should have been enough to guarantee promotion. But successive 2-0 defeats at Halifax and Rochdale proved crucial and City took the title by three points after a charge to the line.

The Millers also made a minor piece of history as the dust settled on the campaign. They again played in Holland, following the success of the previous year, and became the first English side to play German opposition after the war when they lost 5-1 after a marathon twelve-hour road trip to face Hanover.

The big news that summer was that Ardron moved for a ten-figure fee to Nottingham Forest. After a superb three years, there was little hope of hanging on to his services. Despite combining his playing duties with work on the railways, Ardron had been a sensation, with 233 goals during his time at the club, including 102 in the League and cup following the resumption of the League. He remains Rotherham's greatest all-time striker, and filling his boots once he'd signed for Forest, where he bagged another 123 before hanging up his boots, was nigh impossible for the Millmoor club.

United couldn't mirror the previous three years and in 1949/50 the goals didn't flow as before. They scored ten less than the previous year and a staggering thirty-four less than the 1946/47 season, enough for the team to finish off the pace in sixth. The dawn of the fifties hardly signalled what was to come, with the second half of the 1949/50 season seeing disappointingly mixed fortunes.

But 1950/51 was to be a stellar season for all at Rotherham United.

6

INTO THE GOLDEN ERA

All clubs have their golden era. For Rotherham United, the fifties, even though now disappearing into the mists of time, were theirs.

Reg Freeman had brought in the skilful Jimmy Rudd the previous season, and with Jack Shaw in explosive form up front, it seemed that the Millers had found the right formula. They started by winning 5-4 at Oldham and staked their claim for a promotion place pretty quickly. But it was a record eighteen unbeaten games that saw them soar to the top of the table – and this time they stayed there. Six wins came in the final seven games and a promotion was finally clinched amid jubilant scenes in a 2-0 victory at Lincoln on 30 April. United topped the table by seven points from Mansfield, winning sixteen games at home and a staggering fifteen on the road, scoring 103 goals in the process.

Shaw emerged as the hero. Taking over from Ardron was a big call, but he smashed forty-six League and FA Cup goals that year, including five on a memorable day at Darlington in the cup. The now famous team bus had the registration GET 7, and the Millers promptly did so, winning 7-2 as Shaw scored a nap hand. He also bagged a treble in a 3-1 second-round win at Ardron's Forest – how sweet that result must have been – and was on target again in a 2-1 third-round win over Doncaster in front of a sell-out 22,000 at Millmoor. United bowed out next time at Hull, beaten 2-0 in front of another 50,000 attendance, which included 11,000 travelling fans.

United's sojourn in Division Two was to last for seventeen memorable seasons. After the trials and tribulations of the first quarter of a century since the amalgamation, the Millers arrived in the Football League's second tier for the first time since County's brief reign ended in 1923. But fans' initial worries that the board hadn't invested enough in the squad following promotion were dispelled after Reg Freeman's side made a rock-solid start.

They were heady days at Millmoor, being pitched in against the likes of Sheffield Wednesday and United, Huddersfield, West Ham, Leeds and Everton, although the board decided to stick with the squad from the previous season. Those worries were understandable, given that Rotherham went into the campaign with only fourteen full-time professionals on the books.

A 2-1 defeat at home to Nottingham Forest in the opener failed to attract the expected Millmoor full house – only 18,400 turned up – but the moaners and groaners were silenced when United went to Cardiff for their first away game two days later and won 4-2 against a team that boasted five Welsh internationals. Jack Shaw netted twice on the way to another impressive season's tally. He couldn't quite manage the thirty-seven of the previous year but still bagged twenty-five League and cup goals to give United a splendid spearhead. Rotherham promptly shot up the table with successive home wins over Cardiff and then Doncaster, while a subsequent 4-1 beating of Southampton – the first Millmoor match to be broadcast live on BBC Radio – sent hopes soaring.

What followed was a string of games to send blood-pressure levels on the terraces even higher. It started when 5,000 fans made the short trip to Hillsborough to face a Wednesday side on the way to the eventual championship.

Little Rotherham were no respecter of reputations and, in the first League meeting between the clubs for twenty-nine years, watched by nearly 55,000, Shaw netted a brace and others came from Peter Wragg, Jack Grainger and Charlie Tomlinson in a famous 5-3 win.

It got even better. The following week, Leeds were thumped 4-2 at Millmoor and then West Ham were beaten 2-1. Rotherham were up to second and supporters were even beginning to dream of even higher stations; even more so when, after Barnsley and Blackburn were sent packing 4-0 and 3-0 respectively, plus a 3-2 win at QPR, United beat Notts County 2-0 in front of nearly 21,000 to climb to the top of the table.

They stayed there for three games before the wheels came off with a 5-0 battering at Swansea Town, followed by a Christmas Day 4-0 loss to Birmingham, who completed a quick-fire double at St Andrews the following afternoon.

There was still plenty to shout about, despite the slide down the table: a new record crowd of 25,149 watched a 3-3 draw with Wednesday, Millmoor's capacity having been extended following much-needed work on the Tivoli End, and nearly that figure saw Guest net a double in a 3-1 win over the Blades. The season did peter out with five successive defeats, but a mid-table finish of ninth was perfectly acceptable to the crowd, which averaged almost 18,000 for the season. The upstarts from the Third Division had gatecrashed the party and finished around their South Yorkshire rivals Sheffield United, Doncaster and Barnsley.

The following season brought good news in that Jack Grainger rebuffed a move to newly promoted Wednesday. The winger had forced his way into the England B reckoning but chose to stay at Millmoor. Grainger had the honour of becoming Rotherham's first England cap when he was picked for the B side the following March, playing in a 2-2 draw against Scotland at Hibernian's Easter Road. But Grainger would also play a part in one of United's biggest-ever successes in 1952/53.

That season also brought bad news when manager Freeman announced in August that he was leaving. He had accepted Sheffield United's offer of taking charge at Bramall Lane, but few could complain about his service to the Millers, which spanned twenty-one years as a player and manager. Modern fans will talk of the exploits of Ronnie Moore, but Freeman will go down as one of the most successful Millmoor bosses of all time. He had dragged the club away from potential oblivion to the top of Division Two, all the time operating on tight purse strings, and had developed a cavalcade of talented players.

Andy Smailes was handed the job, with Mark Hooper stepping into his shoes as trainer. Smailes had played for the club in 1929, having joined Rotherham as a centre-half from Bristol City, and he was another stalwart servant. He stayed in charge until October 1958, and was the man who steered the club through the purplest of patches.

United again had plenty to be pleased with in Smailes' first season. Ironically, Rotherham's home form wasn't as punishing and their seven away wins kept them out of trouble. They were hampered by an injury to Shaw before Walter Rickett came in from Wednesday in October to create more avenues of attack, and the side promptly rattled off wins at West Ham, Lincoln and Blackburn to push them up the table.

The club finished twelfth but 1952/53 will be remembered more for their FA Cup exploits. In the third round they struggled past Colchester following a replay, setting them up for a fourth-round trip to the mighty Newcastle United. The cup was practically domiciled in Newcastle in the early fifties. The Geordies celebrated success in the competition in 1951 when they beat Blackpool and they repeated the feat a year later when beating Arsenal.

But then, with Newcastle seemingly marching towards a third triumph, thirteen successive wins under their belts in the competition, along came the upstarts from Rotherham – and on 31 January 1953, the Millers pulled off one of the biggest wins in club history.

The wind howled around St James' Park, trees came crashing down in the North East and so did the home side. Newcastle went in front early in the second half before two goals from Grainger and one from Rickett gave Rotherham a shock 3-1 win. Newcastle was so impressed by Grainger that they offered £30,000 for him straight after the game, but again he chose to stay at Millmoor. The giant-killing heroics ended there though, because Aston Villa came to town in the fifth round and promptly won 3-1.

Heading into 1953/54, the main news from the club was that Millmoor was to be improved. Up to then, Rotherham had come in for severe criticism over the state of their ground, with railway sleepers for terracing and little in the way of spectator facilities. Visitors often complained of the cramped conditions – something that would echo right through the years, culminating in West Ham refusing the use the Millmoor changing rooms when they visited some half a century later. In 1953, it was decided to develop the site in four stages. The main stand side would be concreted, the iron railings that surrounded the pitch were removed in favour of a sectional concrete wall, and work would also take place on the Railway End and towards the entrance of the ground.

The good news on that score was tempered by the loss of Jack Shaw to Wednesday. Shaw had taken on the mantle of goalscorer following the departure of Ardron and he'd done it with aplomb. He didn't want to move to Hillsborough, but the ex-miner was eventually lured to the First Division club for £10,000, seen as a replacement for Derek Dooley, and he spent three seasons with the Owls, scoring twenty-seven goals in sixty-five games before hanging up his professional boots as a thirty-year-old.

It was ironic that, after Ardron's exit, Rotherham went on to grab promotion and, following Shaw's transfer, the club embarked on two sensational seasons. Ronnie Burke came in from Huddersfield and, just as Shaw had done, filled the centre-forward role with style. Ian Wilson also arrived from Chesterfield. A 4-1 home defeat by Blackburn hardly signalled what was to come, and when Rotherham went down 4-2 at Leeds in their next outing the soothsayers were getting ready.

They needn't have bothered. United thrashed West Ham 5-0 next time out, Burke and Wilson netting doubles, and they then beat Birmingham 1-0. Minor hiccups followed with defeats at Forest and West Ham but the Millers then won eight of their next nine games to blast their way to the top of the table.

But, as in the previous campaign, the depth of the squad wasn't enough to cover for injuries and Smailes had to chop and change the side. That bumper run was followed by four straight defeats, and Smailes realised he needed support for Burke and Guest up front, bringing in Jock Henderson from now-defunct Scottish club Third Lanark. He made his debut in a 5-2 thrashing of Derby in December but only managed to score twice in twenty-two consecutive appearances. Still, Rotherham managed to hang on to the coat-tails of the frontrunners, and with eleven games to go they were sixth, just three points behind leaders – and eventual champions – Leicester.

Inconsistency was again their undoing. They crushed Oldham 7-0 and put four goals past Lincoln and Doncaster, but too many defeats on the road saw them finish a best-ever fifth.

If that was an impressive campaign, even better was to follow, and 1954/55 saw perhaps the most absorbing season in the club's history as they came within a whisker of being promoted to the First Division for the only time.

Modern-day fans will argue that Ian Porterfield's 1980/81 side or Ronnie Moore's 2001 heroes were up there with the best, but the old-timers will have none of it. They'll say, and perhaps rightly, that United's class of '55 topped the lot.

They had a new chairman in Reg Cooper, who had been on the board for twenty-five years and replaced octogenarian William Watt, and Cooper went perilously close to seeing the club reach the top flight in his maiden year. It was a season that brought some astonishing results, and a cruel sting in the tail as they just missed out.

United started with six wins in the first seven games, including doing the double over Leeds, and centre-forward Ronnie Burke netting all four in a 4-2 victory over Bury. That took them into second place, and even though the Millers had a few shaky moments, a 2-0 victory over Luton on 25 September took them to the top of the table. It certainly was good news time at Millmoor, especially with the announcement that the Masbrough Street End and the Railway End were to be developed and roofed. On top of that, Jack Grainger was picked for the Football League XI to play the Army, and the national press purred over the style of football being played.

By the time 1955 came around, United were third – with two going up in those days – but January wasn't a good month, and in hindsight two of the results cost them promotion. They were thumped 5-1 at Middlesbrough and then, crucially, lost 4-0 at Luton, the side that eventually pipped them to second place on goal difference.

But seven straight wins kept Rotherham right in the thick of it and they went into the final two games, at Port Vale and at home to Liverpool, knowing that four points would guarantee them promotion.

The match at Vale Park is one that has caused much discussion over the years and heartache for one superb servant of the club – Norman Noble. A kingpin at the heart of the defence, he played over 300 games for the club, but is remembered for one particular moment, in front of a packed house of 25,000 including thousands of anxious Rotherham supporters. With the game goalless, a few minutes into the second half Terry Farmer was downed for a penalty. Noble stepped up to take it, unleashing a terrific shot, but 'keeper Ray King fisted the ball to safety. Soon afterwards Vale scored and, to rub salt into United's wounds, the other results failed to go their way.

That meant they faced Liverpool in the finale at Millmoor and needed to win 16-0 to go above Luton, while hoping that leaders Birmingham would lose in the following midweek at Doncaster. In the end they thrashed the Anfield side 6-1, Ian Wilson netting four, but Birmingham made no mistake at Belle Vue, winning 5-1. United, Luton and City all finished on fifty-four points, the Millers agonisingly missing out on goal average. Nobby Noble went to his grave in 1973 carrying the burden of that penalty miss. He shouldn't have because he had been one of the Millers' best-ever clubmen.

One-by-one the players from the golden generation left and the rest of the fifties failed to live up that early promise. In 1955/56 it proved too much to ask for the same prolific form as the previous year. One win in the first eleven games set the tone; attendances dropped, and Andy Smailes failed in a bid to bring Jack Shaw back to the club from Wednesday to try and pep things up.

They did win 2-0 at Hillsborough, Keith Bambridge and Ian Wilson scoring, but seven successive defeats at the end – just 5,415 watching the finale against Swansea Town – saw them finish a disappointing fourth from the bottom.

It wasn't much better in 1956/57. Smailes gave youth a fling with no major signings that year and Gladstone Guest left for Gainsborough Trinity. Guest was one of the Rotherham greats, leading his home-town club through one of the best periods in their history and scoring a record 130 goals. His achievements were enough for the town to award the honour of naming a bus after him, some forty years after he hung up his boots! That gave him as much pleasure as banging in the goals during his playing days.

Rotherham started in 1956 by losing 4-0 at home to Sheffield United, and by September they were stuck at the bottom. Results slowly began to turn around, starting with a 5-1 win at Notts County, and in December United went to Bramall Lane and promptly won 7-2 thanks to goals from Bambridge (2), John Slater (2), Grainger (2) and Ken Keyworth. That was their first-ever League game under floodlights. The next game, they thrashed Bristol City 6-1, but more defeats saw them slip back down, and it seemed as though the bad old ways on the financial front had returned when they put Grainger, Frank Marshall and Keyworth up for sale. The club was struggling for cash and revealed that it couldn't pay its way. Rotherham lost £7,000 that year and finished a lowly seventeenth.

By the time 1957/58 came around, Grainger had moved on to Lincoln and Jack Selkirk had also left, while United suffered another blow when Bambridge was called up for National Service. Bambridge was one of the great characters at Millmoor and tells some great stories, such as the time the players were one by one falling ill and the club was left with a handful of fit players. That was until they realised that the refurbished dressing rooms had been given a lick of lead paint. Scrapers out and problem solved.

In came Barry Webster and Keith Kettleborough was given his chance. After a poor start, Smailes signed several newcomers including Ken Twidle, Glyn Jones and Albert Broadbent from Wednesday, with Peter Johnson heading in the opposite direction. Results ebbed and flowed as Rotherham again flirted with the lower end of Division Two. They then shipped six at Leyton Orient, lost 4-1 at home to Ipswich and were clobbered 6-1 at Bramall Lane. But the worst was to come the following week when the Millers were caned 8-0 at West Ham. There was some respite, as good wins over Barnsley and Swansea kept them out of the relegation squabble, only for United to lose 4-0, 5-0 and 5-1 against Charlton, Blackburn and Charlton again.

Again, the main satisfaction was avoiding relegation, with Smailes having had to chop and change the team perhaps more than in any other season to date, and they did ship a record 101 goals.

That flirtation with relegation was repeated in 1958/59. It started with a 6-1 drubbing at Bristol City and, after a string of bad results, Andy Smailes resigned after a 1-1 draw with Orient in October. He had been with the club as player, trainer and manager since 1929 and, at sixty-three, decided it was time for a new face. Tom Johnson eventually took over, with Rotherham having slumped to the bottom of the table by the time December came around. They were still there at the end of February and the situation looked perilous but Johnson took the bull by the horns and the side did eke out enough points to finish third from the bottom, just a point above Grimsby.

With finance still a problem, Johnson set about overhauling the club as 1960 loomed, putting the emphasis on youngsters as he set up two new youth teams that would go on to produce the players of the future.

Right: The Merry Millers board receive the deeds to Millmoor in 1948 from the Midland Railway Company.

Below: Gladstone Guest fires Rotherham's second goal in a 3-0 win at Lincoln in 1951, the victory giving them the Division Three (North) title.

The 1951 Division Three (North) title-winning team.

The 1955 golden generation team, which went so close to reaching the First Division.

Above left: Manager Andy Smailes, who also played for United in 1929.

Above right: Fifties star Jack Grainger.

Below right: Manager Jack Mansell.

Above: Millmoor action from 1960.

Below: The 1959/60 team.

7

WHEN UNITED BEAT
THE MIGHTY ARSENAL

Despite the financial hardship, Johnston was given cash to bring in striker Bill Myerscough from Aston Villa, while veteran Danny Williams began to wind down his playing career after a magnificent fifteen years at the club. Williams played a massive 461 times for the club, only being surpassed by Paul Hurst some fifty years later. Born in Maltby, he was a Rotherham lad through and through and turned down the chance to play at the likes of the mighty Arsenal to stay with his home-town club.

They started well, losing just two of their first twenty-two games, enough to have the terraces bristling with optimism once again. The key was that Johnson wanted a settled side and heading into Christmas they were second. The Millers beat eventual champions Aston Villa 2-1 in front of over 20,000 at Millmoor, sending hopes soaring, but Johnston's squad just couldn't keep it up. Back-to-back festive defeats against Middlesbrough heralded a mixed run and they eventually finished a creditable eighth.

But 1960 was the year most remembered for one particular series of games. They were drawn against Arsenal in the FA Cup third round and, in the first game at Millmoor, in front of a sell-out crowd, it looked as though they were on the way to a quick exit as the Gunners shot into a 2-0 lead.

Brian Sawyer, being watched by several top clubs, pulled one back, and then Myerscough fired home a penalty to earn Rotherham a replay at Highbury. That one ended 1-1 on an icy pitch, Webster hitting an equaliser, which meant a third game. In those days a coin was tossed and whoever won could choose a venue. Rotherham's chairman Reg Cooper called correctly and picked out Hillsborough. The weekend before, United had ignominiously lost 2-1 at Scunthorpe, but no one could envisage what would follow two days later.

Around 56,000 packed into the ground and, on a famous night, Rotherham gave Arsenal a football lesson. Kettleborough hit the opener after just seven minutes and, with Rotherham rampant, they made it 2-0 when Sawyer struck in the fifteenth minute. That's how it stayed after 138,000 fans had watched the three games with the 57,598 at Highbury remaining the highest crowd ever to watch a Millers' game. It meant they faced Brighton in the fourth round, and in a poetic twist, they also needed three games. The first two were drawn – Brighton chose Highbury for the third game and promptly won 6-0!

The sixties saw United become firmly established as a solid Division Two outfit. In 1960/61 they lost Myerscough to Coventry, started well by beating Southampton at home in the opener thanks to a lone Alan Kirkman goal, and throughout the season just managed to keep their heads above water. They also lost Keith Kettleborough, an inside-forward that had made his debut for his home-town team in 1955. He was sold to Sheffield United for £12,000 in December, with some of the money being spent on bringing in Don Weston from Birmingham, and he quickly became a crowd favourite after scoring the only goal of the game against Liverpool at Christmas on his home debut. Rotherham finished fifteenth, but the season was again remembered more for cup exploits than the League programme.

This time it was the new League Cup. Rotherham started with a 2-1 win at Leicester in October and they then dumped out Bristol Rovers 2-0 in the second round. The same score saw them then oust Bolton Wanderers at Burnden Park, while United booked their semi-final ticket by thumping Portsmouth 3-0. The Millers faced Third Division Shrewsbury Town in the last four shootout, winning 3-2 at home in the first leg with two goals from Sawyer and one from Kirkman. Eight days later the sides met again at the Gay Meadow and Weston's extra-time goal gave them a 1-1 draw and booked their place in the first-ever final.

In those days, the League Cup was treated as an irrelevance by many of the top clubs and some refused to take part. Designed as a floodlit competition – the Millers had switched theirs on for the 23 November tie against Bristol, although the inaugural game under lights had been a reserve match against Darlington two days earlier – it was only when automatic entry to the UEFA Cup was promised to the winners that the full League membership took part.

But, nevertheless, Rotherham was there and rightly took their place in the history books – but only after controversy over the staging of the final against Aston Villa.

The first leg was pencilled in for Monday 1 May at Millmoor but Villa's semi against Burnley became a drawn-out three-game affair before the Midlanders won 2-1; by then it had been decided to hold the game over until the start of the following season. Rotherham understandably objected; after all, they had sold their ticket allocation and were faced with offering refunds while there were strong suggestions that Villa should forfeit their place in the final.

Into 1961/62, the League campaign started with a 2-1 win at Stoke that warmed the team up nicely for the final first leg at Millmoor three days later. Just over 12,000 watched the game; there would undoubtedly have been more had the game been played on time, with over 13,000 having watched the semi against Shrewsbury. Kirkman and Webster gave Rotherham a 2-0 advantage and they headed to Villa Park on 5 September with high hopes.

In a game that saw fast end-to-end football in front of 31,000 fans, Villa hit the visitors with two quick second-half goals. Don Weston went close with three good chances but the tie went into extra time, and with ten minutes left Peter McParland broke Rotherham hearts with the winner, in off the underside of the bar.

Nevertheless, it gave the Millers a flavour for the new competition, and that year they also made it all the way through to the fifth round before bowing out to Blackburn Rovers. In the League, Rotherham climbed to third by the end of November. They battered Bristol Rovers 4-0, Kirkman netting twice en route to becoming the season's top scorer with twenty-two, but on the downside let in five at Scunthorpe and Walsall.

By March, Rotherham were still fifth and were hopeful of putting in a strong promotion challenge – but then the wheels really came off. If United's history had been peppered with inconsistency, this was a slide that took some beating.

After beating Orient 2-1 on 8 March, United then lost nine of their next ten games. It was hard to stomach for many fans, especially after the early season promise, and crowds dropped alarmingly. Just 3,492 watched them draw at home to Luton and manager Johnston was forced, particularly after chairman Reg Cooper intervened, to drop experienced players such as Kirkman, Weston, Lol Morgan and 'keeper Roy Ironside. Weston and Morgan were transfer listed at their own request, while Johnston's response to fans' complaints was that the supporters' expectations were too high, considering the number of youngsters in the team, which finished ninth. But any transfer business that summer was put on hold when Johnston was allowed to join Grimsby and Danny Williams, who just weeks earlier had said he was leaving the club, was put in charge of the team. Williams was also keen on youth development – the Millers had to be because there was little spare cash around – and he brought in Chris Rabjohn, Barry Lyons and Harold Wilcockson while youngsters such as Frank Casper were given a chance.

The 1962/63 season started with defeat at home to newly relegated Chelsea, but four successive wins perked up enthusiasm on the terraces and crowds returned to double figures while 20,000 saw a thrilling 2-1 win over Leeds. Perhaps it was down to high expectations and the inability to keep a small squad performing highly for so long, but again the results began to fade. Weston moved to Leeds and Brian Sawyer to Bradford while new recruit Hugh McIlmoyle didn't last long, and after expressing a wish to move south ended up at Carlisle!

There were high spots as Rotherham finished safely in fourteenth, notably the form of young Albert Bennett. Just seventeen when he joined the Millers, Bennett went on to become one of the club's most successful strikers. He scored twenty-three goals in twenty-nine appearances in his first full season, including two in a 5-0 victory at Bury and a brace in a 4-1 beating of Middlesbrough. Bennett went on to score another thirty-six times over the ensuing two years, before increasing interest from the First Division teams ended with him joining Joe Harvey's Newcastle for a then record £27,000. He was also the only Miller to gain England under-23 honours.

One lifeline for the club had been Rotherham Sportsmen's Association, which had pumped thousands into the coffers over several years. In 1962 they again raised £13,000, which gave the club a profit of £10,000, but didn't mask the fact that trading alone was still difficult. Chairman Cooper wanted an average crowd of 13,000 and he warned that if attendances remained below that – they had slipped back to less than 10,000 – then players would have to be sold.

The 1963/64 campaign started badly. Three successive defeats at Bury and Leeds and at home to Manchester City gave the moaners plenty of fuel, but they were made to eat their words as the Millers went on to finish seventh. That was despite Alan Kirkman having been sold to Newcastle for £12,000, after scoring sixty-three League and cup goals in his six seasons with the club, but the young United side made amends. Danny Williams showed plenty of faith in the new crop and there was plenty of optimism that they could go on and emulate the achievements of the side from a decade earlier – if not exceed them.

By 1963, Rotherham's side bristled with young home-grown talent, such as South Yorkshire men Frank Casper, Brian Tiler, Ian Butler and Barry Lyons. Striker Casper had made eight League appearances in 1962/63 and added another eleven the following year before going on to be a starring marksman in the mid-sixties. He had to work hard to earn his place in the team with Albert Bennett and Ken Houghton restricting his appearances. Tiler made just one appearance in 1962/63 in midfield but boss Williams saw his talent as a striker emerge on the training ground and gave him his chance. Rotherham-born Tiler grabbed it with both hands. He made forty-three League and cup appearances in 1963/64, scoring twenty-two goals from the centre-forward berth. The following season, Casper was less prolific, scoring just eight times in all competitions and that led Williams to switch him back to left-half, where he became a mainstay until leaving for Aston Villa in December 1969. Tiler spent four productive years at Villa Park before wrapping up his career at Carlisle, having a brief sojourn with Portland Timbers in the USA in 1976 and eventually taking over as managing director at Bournemouth. He was tragically killed in a car crash on the outskirts of Rome in 1990, in which then Cherries manager Harry Redknapp was injured.

Young Barry Lyons also came through the junior ranks to shine in 1963/64. A flying winger, he provided many of the ninety goals – more than any of the promoted teams – for the strikers as Rotherham soon got over their poor start, particularly at home. They thumped Bury 6-2 with Ken Houghton grabbing a hat-trick en route to his twenty-one goals and also crushed Charlton 5-0, with Tiler hitting a double.

United won fourteen of their twenty-one home games that year, but on the road it was a different matter and had their away form been better (it took until December before they registered their first victory away from Millmoor with a 4-1 swamping of Derby at the Baseball Ground), they could have mounted a realistic promotion challenge instead of finishing seventh. Underlining Williams' insistence on youth, when the Millers faced Portsmouth in February the entire team had been home-grown.

In the cup, the Millmoor Babes almost pulled off one of the upsets of the season when they drew First Division big guns Burnley in the third round. United drew 1-1 at Turf Moor in the first game and then 23,813 saw them take a 2-1 lead against a side packed with internationals, Lyons netting both – only for the cruellest of luck to strike. With twenty minutes to go and Rotherham on top, Colin Clish broke a leg and, with no subs in those days, Burnley took full advantage to level in the seventy-seventh minute, snatching a winner four minutes from the end.

United stuck with the same squad for 1964/65, even though the bank balance showed a healthy profit from the previous season. Into the 1965/66 season, and Rotherham's youngsters certainly ruffled a few feathers. They started like an express train with five wins in their first seven games, and when Ken Houghton hit the only goal of the game on 15 September it lifted the Millers into top spot. A string of away defeats – and again it was the form on the road that let them down – saw Rotherham slip down to fifth, but it was so tight at the top end that when Houghton struck a hat-trick in a 3-1 win over Cardiff in mid-October they were back in the box seat. A month later, though, and the Millers were down in mid-table, a run of eight defeats in ten away from Millmoor being the prime cause, including a 6-1 drubbing at Southampton. Injuries had played their part and manager Williams had to move into the transfer market to pep up his side. Lanky striker John Galley, born in nearby Clowne, was signed from Wolves for £10,000 and his impact was immediate. Aerial battler Galley, the perfect target man, scored a hat-trick on his debut in a 5-3 win at Coventry and went on to score nine times in his eighteen League and cup appearances.

However, through the exit door in January went Ian Butler and Ken Houghton, both to Hull City, but better news for supporters was that Albert Bennett's expected move to Newcastle didn't materialise.

Williams brought in John Hellawell and Robin Hardy, but things weren't all sweetness and light behind the scenes. The manager, who had repeatedly fought off attempts to sign his young guns, understandably wasn't happy. After the Millers held First Division Wolves to a 2-2 draw at Molineux in the FA Cup fourth round, they lost 3-0 in the replay in front of 25,105 fans; the next day Williams handed in his resignation, while a double bombshell came with a transfer request from captain Peter Madden. Williams' reason was that he wanted to devote more time to his family and intended moving to the South Coast. He did stay on until the end of the season, when he was appointed Swindon manager in June, while a replacement was quickly singled out in the shape of Jack Mansell. In the meantime, Rotherham's season tailed off and they eventually finished fourteenth, which was a disappointment after the team's promising start.

Mansell, who was then thirty-seven, was a former Sheffield Wednesday coach and had been in charge at Dutch team Telstar. One of his first jobs was to allow Bennett to make his move to St James' Park for £27,000 (around £425,000 in today's terms) meaning he had to find a replacement for a player who had scored seventy goals, including twenty-four in his final season, in 121 appearances for the 1965/66 campaign.

Teenager Les Chappell was given a run by Mansell in a pre-season tour of Holland, and the manager was so impressed that the Nottingham-born youngster was thrown straight into the first team. Chappell became near ever-present and was the first man to become a Millers sub, the twelfth man having been introduced that year, when he came on for Keith Pring in a 4-0 defeat at Middlesbrough.

The Millers started brightly, despite a 2-1 defeat against Bristol City. Mansell opted to play attractive football and the goals certainly flowed. They lost 6-4 at home to Cardiff and humiliatingly went down 6-1 at Bury, conversely sticking a half-dozen past Preston on the day when Roy Lambert was sold to Barnsley. By then, mid-October, the Millers were sitting nicely in seventh, which is where they were going into the New Year and where they stayed until the end of the season.

But the major talking point of 1965/66 – perhaps the entire decade – was the FA Cup fourth-round thriller against mighty Manchester United. It was to be one of the biggest and most controversial games in their history.

The Millers had disposed of Third Division Southend in the third round, due to an own goal, and there was great excitement when the draw paired them with Matt Busby's Red Devils at Old Trafford. Mansell's side played their hearts out in front of 54,000 on 12 February, both sides hitting the woodwork, but both unable to make the breakthrough as Rotherham defended stubbornly against the star-studded giants. Around 12,000 Millers fans made the trip. It meant they had to do it all again in front of a full house at Millmoor, Busby fielding a full-strength side – but this time it was a game that was the subject of arguments for years to come.

Rotherham were denied what appeared to be a perfectly good goal in the thirty-second minute when Chappell scrambled the ball home, after Galley had crossed the ball from the left. Referee Jack Taylor had no hesitation in signalling a goal and even 'keeper Harry Gregg kicked the ball down the middle to the centre-spot. But the home fans' cheers were stifled when, after a lengthy consultation with a linesman, Taylor changed his mind, disallowed the goal and awarded a free-kick to Manchester for what, he explained later, was offside. Taylor's name was mud in Rotherham for many years afterwards.

Shortly before half-time, Manchester had another let-off. This time, Gregg could only punch out a header from Chappell. The ball struck Galley and was on its way into goal when Nobby Stiles pulled it back, but it looked as though it might have crossed the line before the England World Cup star's clearance hit the underside of the bar and the ball was eventually scrambled away. The Millers played some lovely football that night but eventually bowed to a goal from John Connelly five minutes from the end.

Busby had this to say of the young Millers' team:

> We have been impressed with the display of Rotherham United in both matches, and if they continue to produce such football they must have a bright future, because they are all very young. We have had two magnificent games, not only from the point of view of quality football but also from the sportsmanship displayed.

Off the field, things were also happening. Eric Purshouse had already taken over as chairman from Reg Cooper with the declaration that he would keep a tight financial grip on the club. He certainly did that and, even though Mr Purshouse was pilloried in future years, there's no doubt that he built a solid base at the bank, whereas in previous decades Rotherham had suffered from shaky foundations.

Mr Purshouse was also at the helm of some ambitious plans to develop Millmoor. New shares were issued and plans were mooted of a redesign for the ground, which ambitiously included double-decker stands around the pitch. Of course, they never materialised, although a new state-of-the-art gym was built at a cost of £35,000 and the Millmoor Lane side was finally concreted.

The 1966/67 season opened brightly with a 3-1 win over Millwall, but as part of the recurring theme over the years, Rotherham couldn't keep up the standards of the previous season and fell onto a slippery slope that would take them out of Division Two. The standard was set after that win over Millwall and they won only one of their next seven games, a 4-2 victory over Plymouth with Lyons scoring twice. Chappell and Galley proved to be the mainstays up front in an otherwise goal-shy side, eventually scoring sixteen and seventeen goals respectively, while Casper struggled to make an impact. It was a campaign punctuated by just enough wins to keep them above the relegation scrap, although there were real fears mid-season after a 2-1 win over Blackburn in early December proved to be their only success until a 3-2 triumph over Birmingham almost two months later.

The highlight of the year again came in the League Cup, a 1-0 win at Hillsborough thanks to Casper, before they bowed out in the next round against Northampton. United eventually finished six points above the relegation places. It was enough for safety but too close for comfort, and it was a precursor for another much talked about campaign which ultimately ended in disaster.

The close season saw Rotherham sign defender Billy Thompson from Newcastle to prop up the strength in the side, but almost immediately Jack Mansell quit the club. He probably saw the writing on the wall, and when an offer came to manage Boston Beacons in the fledging North American Soccer League he took it.

As if that wasn't bad enough, Casper soon followed him out of the Millmoor exit door, sold to Burnley by the board for £27,000. Casper had given sterling service to the club and would do likewise for the Clarets, where he went on to serve for two decades as a player (scoring nearly a goal every three games), coach and eventually manager.

Fred Green was brought in as caretaker and held the post until November when Rotherham United made the football world sit up and take notice.

The 1967/68 season started badly. Very badly. The disrupted Millers, playing in a new all-red strip for the first time, plunged to the foot of the table after starting with a 3-0 home defeat to Crystal Palace. They were then beaten 3-1 in successive games at Aston Villa and at home to Derby and QPR before being walloped 4-1 at Carlisle. The board knew they had to act fast and offered the manager's job to Chesterfield's Jim McGuigan, who promptly turned it down. Rotherham stopped the tide when a David Chambers goal was enough to beat fellow strugglers Plymouth at Home Park before Chappell, Galley and Laurie Sheffield netted in a 3-2 victory at home to Cardiff, watched by just 5,541 spectators. A 1-1 draw at Portsmouth made it three without defeat but United were struggling, and they then lost five of their next six games.

In late November, the Rotherham board announced that Tommy Docherty was taking over the hot seat. If Eric Purshouse and his board wanted to make headlines and rekindle the Rotherham flame, they'd done a good job. Docherty had left Chelsea a month earlier under a cloud after six years at Stamford Bridge, where he'd taken up the managerial reins following a star-studded playing career and built a side which would go on to international success.

It wasn't that Docherty left Chelsea for South Yorkshire. Not at all. But when Rotherham heard he was out of work, they stepped in. Docherty fancied the challenge and within days of his nigh-sensational appointment he promised to take United out of Division Two – he did that alright, but it was the wrong way.

Rotherham were propelled into the national news. It was a big deal for the club, his contract being almost as good as that at Stamford Bridge should he achieve promotion. He moved quickly to bring in Johnny Quinn from Hillsborough for a princely £27,500 (around £375,000 in today's terms) and then sold John Galley to Bristol City without even having seen the striker play. Ironically, he scored a hat-trick in his first game for City and his goals were enough to save his new club from relegation as Docherty failed.

The Scot's arrival at Millmoor pumped up enthusiasm in the town. His first game in charge was at Millwall, where the team drew 0-0, followed by a home game with Hull City, where Quinn's debut was marked by 15,000 packing into Millmoor, only for United to lose 3-1. They then lost 3-1 at Blackburn, 1-0 at Crystal Palace and 2-0 at home to Villa with 6,000 fewer in the ground than the Hull game, and the honeymoon was soon over as the Millers went seven games without a win.

The deadlock was broken as defender Colin Clish scored the only goal against Preston, with experienced Scot Jim Storrie making his debut up front after signing from Aberdeen. Days later Docherty signed the young David Watson from Notts County. The man who went on to become a bulwark in England's defence in the 1980s, and was perhaps Rotherham's best-ever product made his debut on the left wing at QPR in the first game of the New Year, could do nothing to stop his side from crashing 6-0.

Docherty chopped and changed his permutations: players such as Harold Wilcockson, Laurie Sheffield, Colin Clish, Chris Rabjon and John Haselden were shipped out, and the manager also signed the likes of Dennis Leigh and Graham Watson while giving chances to junior products such as Trevor Swift, Steve Downes, John Shepherd, Neil Hague and Lee Brogden. After the Loftus Road disaster, Rotherham drew their next four games and then drew some hope in the relegation fight by winning three on the trot, beating Huddersfield, Bolton and fellow strugglers Plymouth, drawing with Birmingham and then winning 1-0 at Bristol with young hotshot Downes netting the only goal. Rotherham gave themselves a fighting chance but then three defeats, coupled with Bristol City and Preston winning their games in hand, left them back in the mire. After seventeen successive seasons in the second tier, United were relegated.

Sandwiched in the middle of it all was a terrific FA Cup run that saw wins over Wolves and then at Villa before they bowed out in the fifth round for only the second time in their history, losing 2-0 after a replay against Leicester. It gave supporters some hope, especially with Docherty having repeated his achievement at Chelsea by developing some highly promising young players and not being afraid to blood them in the high-pressure fight against relegation. More new faces were brought in by Docherty: Alan Gilliver from Blackburn and the Doc's former Scottish international team-mate Graham Leggatt from Birmingham. But any high hopes were soon tempered, even though Rotherham drew their opener at Orient and then beat Tranmere 4-1 with Leggatt and Downes each scoring twice. Goalie Alan Hill went to Nottingham Forest and the Doc signed another seasoned player in Jim Furnell from Arsenal to replace him, while another youngster, Trevor Womble, was also given his chance. Eight games without a win kept them out of the promotion reckoning, and in the middle of that mini-run United were shocked when Dochery announced he was leaving in early November. He had insisted he'd be at Millmoor for five years, but announced that the job offer made by QPR was too good to turn down. He was to last just twenty-eight days at the London club before walking out after a row over the signing of United skipper Brian Tiler. Rotherham quickly stressed that he wouldn't be returning to Millmoor.

Docherty promptly joined Villa and got his wish when he signed Tiler for £33,000. Docherty's wheelings and dealings had left Rotherham with a deficit of £42,000 and worries that the prudence under the Purshouses was about to end. Ironically, Tiler's sale helped plug that particular financial gap.

The 1968/69 season petered out as Rotherham finished a disappointing eleventh, with first-team coach Jim McAnearney taking charge and bringing in winger Jimmy Mullen from Charlton and Billy Griffin.

8

STUMBLING THROUGH THE SEVENTIES

If the sixties hadn't exactly been swinging for Rotherham, the seventies echoed past years in that the team stumbled to relegation and flirted with promotion. Consistent it wasn't.

The 1969/70 season began with McAnearney at the helm, and a warning from Eric Purshouse that finances would be tight after the free rein given to Docherty the previous year when it came to negotiating with players. Rotherham beat Bury 4-3 in the opener, with David Bentley scoring twice, but that was followed by a five-match run without a win. This set the agenda for another unremarkable season as they eventually finished eleventh, although they did go eighteen games unbeaten in mid-campaign, albeit with ten of the games drawn.

McAnearney signed a young Neil Warnock from Chesterfield and also brought in John Fantham from Wednesday for a cut-price £6,000 – not surprising because the Owls clearly had their eye on both Dave Watson, by then a mainstay at centre-half, and the highly rated Steve Downes. Rotherham turned down a £44,000 bid for Watson and he continued in a Millers shirt for the whole campaign, although they did relent when Wednesday upped their initial offer of £30,000 for Downes to £40,000.

Meanwhile, the youth production line continued to churn out young talent when seventeen-year-old Trevor Phillips made his debut in a 5-0 drubbing of Barrow, and off the field there were two other notables. The first was the opening of the plush new Windmill Night Club on the forecourt, which was expected to develop a rich new revenue stream for the club, while United's first major title came when they won the only staging of the BBC's Kop Choir competition. The fans were in full voice when the Beeb recorded at the 1-1 draw with Halifax in March and it was enough to give the club the title – ahead of the famed Liverpool Kop – and earn a section of the supporters a trip to the European Cup final in Milan.

The young Millers team performed better in 1970/71, ten draws on home soil being the reason they didn't make more of a challenge at the top end. McAnearney experimented by pushing Watson up front, where he'd started his Millers career, and he responded by scoring a hat-trick, a season's best 5-1 victory against Rochdale. That perked up Sunderland's interest even more: the Wearsiders had been keeping a close eye on the big man as well as England youth international Phillips, and in November they made their move.

They made their move by putting £100,000 on the table, and Watson played his last game in a 4-1 FA Cup win at Grantham on 12 December. He played 121 times for Rotherham and, in a five-year career at Roker Park, made 177 appearances, helped Sunderland to their famous 1973 FA Cup final win and made his England debut. His international career continued after a £275,000 move to Manchester City, and he finished his England career with fourteen caps. He also went on to play for such as Werder Bremen, Southampton, Stoke and Derby before his League career ended at Notts County in 1985.

Watson's departure was quickly forgotten once the draw for the FA Cup third round was made, providing Rotherham with the highlight of the year – against the mighty Leeds United. Crowds queued for hours for tickets for the 24,000 sell-out, but it twice fell victim to the weather before the game was finally played on 9 January.

Leeds fielded a full-strength team and were lucky to escape with a 0-0 draw, John Fantham missing a terrific chance and England World Cup legend Jack Charlton being lucky to stay on the field after an agricultural challenge on David Bentley. He also squared up to the diminutive Phillips, who had been a nuisance all game.

The replay at Elland Road, just two days later, was initially postponed and a week later the sides met again – and what a scare the Millers gave Don Revie's star-studded side. Peter Lorimer scored first, but Trevor Womble and Bentley put United in front at half-time to stun the bulk of the 36,000 crowd. Lorimer and Johnny Giles struck in the second half to spare Leeds' blushes but the Millers took bags of credit. McAnearney made several moves in the transfer marker, bringing in Welsh international Ray Mielczarek from Huddersfield, Eddie Ferguson from Dumbarton and striker Carl Gilbert from Bristol Rovers.

The Millers finished eighth and that was enough to raise expectations the following season. They started 1971/72 with a win-some, lose-some culture before a surprise 4-2 home defeat at the hands of fancied Brighton was followed by a fourteen-game unbeaten run. Gilbert initially struggled to make headway, scoring once in the first four games, before exploding into action by scoring the lot in a 4-0 thrashing of Swansea. The Millers pulled off a shock 2-1 win at table-topping Aston Villa before McAnearney signed forward Bobby Ham from Preston. He went on to form a formidable strike partnership with Gilbert, and United looked a good bet to challenge for promotion. But the wheels came off when they failed to win a game in March and they eventually finished fifth, ten points off the promotion pace.

Going into 1972/73, injury-wracked Johnny Quinn was freed with few incomings and Rotherham started well, with three wins in their opening four League games, including a 7-0 thrashing of Port Vale, and the blond bomber Gilbert netted a hat-trick. It put them in top spot for the first time since 1964 and, after losing at Wrexham, United promptly won their next three.

But the season fell apart when they lost 1-0 at home to Halifax, the first of eight games without a win. That included a horrendous Tuesday night in October when Bournemouth came to town. Gilbert put the home side ahead but the visitors equalised. In only the eleventh minute, goalkeeper Jim McDonagh had to go off after a collision and, as the drama unfolded, Gilbert had to go in goal. He let three quick goals in to leave the Cherries 3-1 up at half-time. They shipped another four in the second period to lose 7-2, Gilbert swapping the goalkeeper's jersey with Mick Leng to go back up front and score a second!

McAnearney signed gritty midfielder Billy Wilkinson and seasoned striker Mike O'Grady to pep Rotherham up, while young local lad John Breckin was brought out of the junior ranks to make his debut. Breckin would go on to be one of Rotherham's best-ever servants. But in February they lost all five games, conceding four three times at Bournemouth, Plymouth and Port Vale – and that after being beaten 4-1 at home by Notts County at the end of January. The alarm bells were well and truly clanging, and with six games left they were stuck in a seven-club fight to avoid the drop. They won 1-0 at Bolton, which was followed by similar results against Rochdale and Southend to give them hope, but the bad news was that everyone else picked up points.

A 2-1 defeat at Blackburn plunged United right back in it, and when they lost 3-2 at home to Oldham it meant they had to beat York at home in the final game to avoid the drop. They didn't, City won 2-1 and with the Shaymen winning their finale it meant Rotherham dropped into the Fourth Division for the first time in their history. They notched forty-one points, the same as Halifax, Watford and, crucially, York, and went down on goal difference.

The close season saw a double blow. Firstly McAnearney resigned, with Jim McGuigan taking over, and it was also announced that the club lost a worrying £63,000.

But Rotherham's stay in the fourth tier was to be brief. In similar fashion to when they slumped out of Division Two, Rotherham were expected to challenge for promotion straight away. The 1973/74 season started amazingly with an astonishing 8-1 victory at Crewe Alexandra – still the Millers' record away win – coming just three games in as Trevor Phillips netted a hat-trick. But that was the last victory for five games and Rotherham continued to struggle through the campaign. They were inconsistent throughout and gates slumped alarmingly, just 2,259 watching a 1-1 draw with Brentford in March, in which eighteen-year-old Richard Finney made his debut while still at school.

United slid to third from the bottom and anxiety about re-election surfaced for the first time in forty years. A new record-low crowd of 1,945 turned up to watch a 3-2 win over Chester, but don't forget that this was all during tough economic times with the 1974 miners strike, a three-day week hitting people in the pockets and restrictions over when games could be played. Floodlights were out, hence only 2,240 turning up to watch the derby with Doncaster on a Tuesday afternoon while clubs were allowed to play on a Sunday for the first time.

Even though it was a miserable time, three wins in the last four games saw the Millers finish fifteenth. The board realised that things needed to change, especially after a loss of £56,000 was announced.

McGuigan moved quickly, bringing in hard man Tommy Spencer on a free, after he earlier signed Jimmy Goodfellow and Bob Delgado. They got off to a good start, winning 3-0 at Torquay through Finney, Phillips and another youth product, Alan Crawford, who had broken into the first team the previous season. They lost just once in the first ten games and then went on another run to climb to third in the table. Once again, with youth having its fling as half of the sixteen players who featured that year had come off Rotherham's production line, promotion began to be the buzzword.

This time United didn't disappoint. A nine-game unbeaten run early in the new year set them on their way, ironically after non-League Stafford Rangers had embarrassingly dumped them out of the FA Cup in a third-round replay at Millmoor. Dick Habbin was signed from Reading to add to the strike force after Ron Wigg was sold to Grimsby. Habbin scored ten times in his twenty-one appearances, including a double as they beat Rochdale 3-1 to seal promotion with two games to go. The first-ever civic reception for the team was well deserved.

Back in Division Three for 1975/76, Rotherham brought in yet another local player when seventeen-year-old Paul Stancliffe took his place in the side for the opener at Brighton, which brought the side back down to earth with a 3-0 defeat. McGuigan had decided, considering that the club lost another £32,000 the previous year, to continue the fruitful grow-your-own policy. Steely defender John Green and playmaker Mark Rhodes were thrown in at the deep end and performed excellently. A string of scouts continued to watch intently as United held their own in tough company, including thumping Malcolm Allison's Crystal Palace 4-1 as Finney hit a double and beating Wednesday 1-0 at Millmoor thanks to a Habbin strike.

McGuigan also pulled off a master stroke when he signed big Dave Gwyther from Halifax for £17,000, helping to alleviate a burgeoning injury crisis that saw Trevor Womble out for the season with knee ligament damage and goalie Jim McDonagh suffer a broken leg at Chesterfield. Former Blades 'keeper Tom McAllister also came to the club.

Those acquisitions had come at a cost: Rotherham, who finished a creditable sixteenth, lost nearly £60,000 and had to appeal to the bank for help. But once the injuries cleared up, McGuigan was left with a strong squad and they very nearly won promotion in a memorable 1976/77 campaign.

The first half of the campaign saw the Millers start superbly, winning their first three games and then, after a couple of blips, going thirteen games without defeat, including a come-from-behind 3-1 victory at Hillsborough at the beginning of November. By the turn of the year, a 4-1 Boxing Day thumping of Northampton had launched them into top spot and just before Easter five wins on the spin kept them in contention.

Three defeats in four saw them left on the fringe, although the 2-1 reverse at Wrexham should have been the game that put them on the road to promotion. They say football can be a cruel game, but what should have been a stellar goal from Rhodes, a pile driver from the edge of the area, was ruled out with a linesman flagging for offside. They player concerned wasn't nearly interfering with play but the goal didn't stand. Rotherham lost, and in the end they missed out on a place in Division Two on goal difference!

As if that wasn't enough, the following week they collapsed 5-1 at lowly Portsmouth. That proved cutting in the final reckoning with Crystal Palace shading by with just three goals as the Millers were left in fourth place!

But that was as good as it got in the seventies.

The following year, struggling with injuries, they forgot the promotion charge and again flirted with relegation. There wasn't much for the fans to shout about, apart from the arrival of young north-easterner Gerry Forrest, an astute signing from minnows South Bank, and another youngster, Peter Nix, making his debut on the left wing after Alan Crawford joined the queue for the treatment table. Rotherham finished twentieth, three points above the drop, a disappointing end to the season seeing them crushed 7-1 by champions-elect Wrexham.

The 1978/79 season brought much of the same. Only three times did they score more than two goals in the League and a final position of seventeenth did bring some stability, with the best action being reserved for the cup competitions.

In the FA Cup, the Millers overcame Workington and Barnsley, a season's best of 15,508 watching the 2-1 replay win over the Reds with Gwyther and Phillips scoring. That brought a third-round draw at Manchester City and they played superbly at Maine Road to earn a 0-0 draw, going mightily close to pulling off a shock win. The sides came back to Millmoor but there was no fairytale, as City stormed into a 3-0 lead before winning 4-2. In the League Cup, the most memorable match of an otherwise forgettable year was a second-round tie against the mighty Arsenal. The Gunners, with a full-strength side including Pat Jennings, Liam Brady, Alan Sunderland and Malcolm MacDonald, expected a cakewalk and led after only seven minutes through Frank Stapleton. But Rotherham didn't give up, as cult hero Gwyther headed home after twenty-five minutes – and two minutes later the ground erupted when John Green nodded his side in front. The Millers were simply superb that night, snuffing out any Arsenal hopes of an equaliser, and just after the hour Richard Finney wrapped up the 3-1 win. It was the night when former England star MacDonald's career effectively ended, as he suffered a knee injury from which he never properly recovered. The glory of that night, though, was soon tempered as Rotherham bowed out 1-0 at Reading in the next round.

That summer, Trevor Phillips was sold to Hull for £70,000 with goalie Tom McAllister going to Blackpool for £45,000. United brought in Rod Fern from Chesterfield – Alan Crawford heading the opposite way – Ken Tiler from Brighton and Billy McEwan from Peterborough. It proved to be another poor season on the field, starting with a crushing 5-1 defeat at Oxford. The Millers stuttered their way through the campaign, putting four past Carlisle and Brentford at home, while being hit for five at Mansfield and Sheffield Wednesday and losing 6-2 at Swindon as the season tailed off to a thirteenth-place finish. Jim McGuigan had left for Stockport mid-season with Barry Claxton taking over on a temporary basis.

Little did fans know that behind the scenes a major change was on the cards as the club moved into the 1980s, and after an initial flurry, it almost cost Rotherham United its very existence.

As the 1979/80 season teetered along, the Purshouse family were becoming tired of personal abuse directed at them by fans who, in turn, were fed up of mediocrity. The Purshouses, Eric and Lewis, had given the club financial stability; they were in the black to the tune of £250,000 when they left, but that wasn't enough for many supporters.

And so in came a certain Anton Johnson, an Essex-based businessman who promised the earth and almost delivered disaster, and eventually became probably the first football chairman to be pursued by the *World in Action* investigative team for what were some shady dealings. There are so many questions still to be answered over the Anton Johnson affair. How, indeed, did he manage to purchase a club which for once in its life looked financially healthy and owned its own ground for a knock-down £62,000?

Johnson took charge in December 1979 and his first job was to bring in former Sunderland hero Ian Porterfield, who was finishing his playing career down the road at Hillsborough, as manager. The thirty-three-year-old, taking his first steps in management, brought in Phil Henson, Vic Halom and 'keeper Graham Brown. Porterfield was raw but ambitious and with Johnson's backing he built one of United's best-ever sides.

9

A BIG HIGH ...
BUT MORE LOWS TO FOLLOW

Ian Porterfield had reached his first target within months of taking charge: saving the Millers from relegation. As he prepared for the 1980/81 season, he brought in Jimmy Mullen from Hillsborough, who was immediately made skipper and became a rock at the heart of defence. Then came the signing of Ronnie Moore from Cardiff for £100,000. That wasn't greeted with overwhelming enthusiasm, especially after he had scored just six times in fifty-six appearances for the Bluebirds – City fans had even had t-shirts made saying 'I Saw Ronnie Moore Score'! That was almost immediately followed by the acquisition of Tony Towner and John Seasman from Millwall for a dual-deal £180,000.

The campaign started with six winless games in the League and League Cup, hardly what was expected of Johnson and Porterfield's new, exciting tenure. But the ball really did start rolling when Moore and Richard Finney netted in a 2-0 victory over Barnsley in front of 10,700 at Millmoor. Even though they lost next time out at Swindon, United then eased to four wins on the spin, including a 2-1 triumph at Bramall Lane. By Christmas, Rotherham were up there at the top end and when they beat Swindon 1-0 thanks to a Mick Gooding goal, it put Porterfield's side top.

Sheffield United were the next visitors and it proved to be a famous victory, one which made fans realise that the current crop of Millers might just achieve something special. The Blades led in the first half, only for Towner to level after seventy minutes. Then, with the seconds ticking down, Towner burst down the right and his cross was punched out by the 'keeper – straight onto Moore's head and, some say with lightning reaction, others say with luck, he buried the winner in front of the Tivoli End.

The Millers went on to put in a stunning finish. Six straight wins included a 3-0 victory over table-top rivals Charlton, and when Fern struck at Carlisle's Brunton Park with four games to go, the 1-0 win was enough to seal promotion. Now the Millers wanted the title – and they got it despite successive away defeats at Brentford and Barnsley, with the Oakwell side also vying for top spot.

In the finale at home to Plymouth, Rotherham needed to win to finish top. But with the game locked at 1-1 with ten minutes to go and Barnsley winning comfortably, it looked as though they'd have to settle for second – until Fern broke clear, fired the ball past the Argyle 'keeper and caused the whole ground to erupt. Moore earned his place in Millers folklore with his twenty-five goals; the team kept a remarkable twenty-six clean sheets and was unbeaten at home.

But history should have told you by now that nothing is straightforward at Rotherham. Within weeks, Porterfield stunned everyone by announcing that he was leaving to join neighbours Sheffield United, who had just slipped down into Division Four after losing at home to Walsall on the day the Millers won the title.

Once again, it left unanswered questions. There was speculation that the links between Rotherham and the Blades were close – too close. Indeed, suggestions later emerged that then Blades chairman Reg Brealey had some form of financial link with Johnson – later fuelled by rock-solid defender Paul Stancliffe and star winger Towner switching to Bramall Lane. Johnson wanted a top-name replacement to lead the Millers into Division Two and advertised nationally with, reportedly, some big names applying including England legend Emlyn Hughes. Hughes was subsequently appointed and went on to steer Rotherham through another astonishing season as, for the first time in a quarter of a century, they came within touching distance of Division One.

He relied on the bulk of the squad that had gained promotion and, despite the trepidation of the challenge ahead, Rotherham got a flier as they walloped Norwich City 4-1 in the opener, with Fern bagging a double. But even though the wheels didn't exactly come off in the next clutch of games, they did look decidedly wobbly. One win in seven saw United slide down the table, while the reliable Jimmy Mullen was allowed to go to Preston with Hughes coming into the side to take the No. 6 shirt.

But they ended the gloomy mini-spell in a way current fans can only dream of – a 6-0 home win over Chelsea with Fern grabbing a hat-trick. Still, results continued to waver and Hughes realised he needed more steel in midfield and signed Gerry Gow from Manchester City for £40,000. Gow wanted to make an impact and did just that on his debut in a midweek game against Derby. Booked after a crunching challenge inside a minute, he did exactly the same two minutes later and was dramatically sent-off! Derby took the lead but battling Rotherham came back to win 2-1, with Moore netting the winner. That was the start of a League record *nine* straight wins for the Millers that included six clean sheets for goalie Ray Mountford. By the time the run ended with a 0-0 draw at home to Newcastle in mid-March – Towner missing an injury time penalty – Rotherham were in the thick of the promotion scramble.

They were beaten next time out at Leicester, but responded by heading to Stamford Bridge and winning 4-1. That was a 10-1 aggregate over the Londoners for the season! They couldn't quite keep pace in the final flurry of a terrific season and eventually finished seventh, four points off promotion.

But crowds were up by over 50 per cent and Rotherham were optimistic that the upward momentum could be continued. Johnson was linked with several other clubs, including troubled Wolves and Derby, but pledged his future to the Millers.

Behind the scenes, though, all was far from well. The rot had started to set in on a decade that saw Rotherham plummet to the brink of extinction.

Heading into 1982/83, Joe McBride was signed from Everton for £50,000, but the Millers started poorly and it wasn't until the fifth game, a 2-1 win over Burnley, that they got off the mark. The first half of the season saw United thumped 5-1 at home by

Newcastle, Kevin Keegan scoring four, while, conversely, they beat Charlton 5-1 with Moore netting a hat-trick. Not only did that performance impress everyone at Millmoor, it did likewise at The Valley, and within a year the big striker went on to become a Charlton player.

By Christmas, when McBride scored a famous goal at Hillsborough to give Rotherham a 1-0 win, Owls 'keeper Bob Bolder being flummoxed when the ball hit a divot and gave McBride an open goal, the Millmoor side found themselves in a comfortable eleventh place. But even though the New Year started well with a win over Charlton, Rotherham then embarked on a punishing twelve-game winless streak that saw them plunge down the table. Ten games into that spell, with speculation mounting about Rotherham's financial situation and talk of Johnson leaving, Emlyn Hughes' brief tenure came to an end.

Hughes made mistakes in his first managerial venture and, perhaps wrongly, tried to create a mini-Anfield at Millmoor. He had a board put up at the top of the players' tunnel stating 'This is Millmoor' mimicking the famous sign at Liverpool and tried to establish a Boot Room culture, but what he failed to realise was that Rotherham wasn't Anfield. Hughes struggled to get to grips with the demands of running a club like the Millers. His appointment, like that of Docherty fifteen years earlier, was a big publicity coup and seemed an ambitious step forward, but it just didn't work out. The final straw came when Rotherham were hammered 4-0 at QPR in mid-March. Hughes was approached in his hotel room after the game by the directors and was asked to resign; the following day he did.

If Hughes' reign was flawed, his successor's was a disaster. Former Grimsby Town boss George Kerr was brought in within days and promptly began dismantling the playing squad, which involved star winger Towner almost immediately leaving for Bramall Lane in a swap deal for Kevin Arnott, while in came Grimsby bit-part players Bobby Mitchell and Paul Friar. After Kerr's arrival, Rotherham won just two of their remaining ten games and went down in the third relegation place. Ironically, Kerr's former club, Grimsby, survived just one position above.

So it was back to Division Three in 1983/84. The new boss signed a raft of players, several coming from Blundell Park, and just four games, which promisingly included three wins, Moore was sold to Charlton.

No longer had the season started than Anton Johnson announced that he was leaving Millmoor. Amid more rumours that Johnson was involved in some shady dealings with other Football League clubs, which eventually sparked the *World in Action* interest, the man who had flamboyantly arrived in town in a helicopter, wore an outrageous fur coat, released his own pop single and always had burly minders with him passed his 52 per cent shareholding to bookmaker Mick McGarry.

In his final months at Rotherham, Johnson was reported to have had controlling interests in three clubs – the Millers, Southend United and AFC Bournemouth – all of whom were in Division Three that season. This raised questions about a breach of League regulations and also potential teeming and labelling of cash and points should one of the three need it. That followed his interest the previous season in both Rotherham and Derby County, including the admission that an £11,000 loan had been made using Rotherham money to Derby, also fighting to stave off relegation, to help pay wages.

Regardless, in the space of three years, Rotherham had gone from having plenty of cash in the bank to being £285,000 in debt. The two years of success had been at an enormous cost, and left the club facing a very difficult future.

Johnson disappeared from the scene but, some thirty years later, journalists at the *Rotherham Advertiser* were astonished when he rang up out of the blue. He was, he said, writing a book about his time in football, but despite some pertinent questions being re-tabled, he again went to ground, never to be heard from again.

That season, as United struggled against relegation straight through to Division Four, crowds dropped to below 4,000 and the team was a shadow of the one that had gone so close to the top flight just a couple of years earlier. They finished a mediocre eighteenth and the one bright spot was the team's form in the League Cup, when they beat top sides Luton, Southampton and Wimbledon before bowing out 4-2 at home to Walsall. By the time 1984/85 came round there was another change of ownership. This time local coach firm owner and staunch fan Syd Wood took over with Graham Humphries as his vice-chairman.

Saddled with debuts of £250,000, Wood's tenure was always going to be difficult. On the pitch, the team stuttered to twelfth place, the lowlight being a 7-0 thrashing at Burnley and defeats in their final five games included a 1-0 home defeat against Cambridge in front of just 1,515 fans, the lowest since 1934.

During the season, new directors were brought in the shape of John Harrison and Ken Booth, while at the end of it, Kerr parted company by mutual consent. He had been in charge in difficult circumstances and had made the best of a bad job, but Kerr presided over a steep downward spiral.

Syd Wood decided he needed a big name and the job went to former Leeds United and England hard man Norman Hunter. He wasn't new to the managerial game, unlike predecessors Porterfield and Hughes, and brought in several new players, with Dean Emerson signing from Stockport, Kevan Smith from Darlington, Tommy Tynan from Plymouth, Daral Pugh from Huddersfield and 'keeper Kelham O'Hanlon from Middlesbrough. But 1985/86 was another mediocre year, Rotherham finishing fourteenth, with star defender Gerry Forrest moving to Southampton for £100,000, and the club launched Millers Mayday to try and bring revenue into the straining coffers.

Hunter again chopped and changed for 1986/87, when the play-offs were introduced for the first time, but it was more of the same. An early season stint of six straight defeats, including a 4-1 home beating by Middlesbrough, saw the team struggling in the bottom half and even in bottom sport after a 5-0 battering at Notts County, but they eventually climbed to finish in fourteenth once again.

In the boardroom, there were depressing days. The club's debt had spiralled to £500,000 and they were losing around £3,000 a week. It was only a £35,000 loan from Rotherham Council that kept the club out of the insolvency courts and staved off approaches by bailiffs to remove equipment to be sold off and pay creditors.

Wood pleaded with the Council to buy the ground and lease it back to the club but they refused, and near the end of the season, with the deficit climbing on a weekly basis to nearly £800,000, they were forced to appoint an administrator. There had been tough times before – and there would be even tougher ones in future – but this was the closest so far that Rotherham United had come to extinction.

Administrator David Stokes worked long and hard to find a solution but the immediate future was secured when United were given leeway by their bank, and local firms C. F. Booth Ltd and Rotherham Engineering Steels stepped in to pay the wages until the end of the season. On 13 May 1987, Ken Booth began his long and often turbulent association with the club. The millionaire scrap dealer wiped off the debts and brought in son-in-law Ron Hull and car dealer Barry Peacock on the board.

That gave everyone more optimism for 1986/87. Hunter brought youth product Nigel Johnson back from his brief, injury-hit spell with Manchester City, with midfielder Tony Grealish also signing from Maine Road. Nevertheless, Rotherham had a traumatic season. Stability had been achieved in the boardroom but on the pitch the team stumbled to just two wins in their first thirteen games. Hunter's side were humbled 7-1 at Sunderland in the Freight Rover Trophy but the worst was to come when they travelled to then non-League Macclesfield in the second round of the FA Cup on 6 December. Rotherham was embarrassingly dumped out 4-0, the sight of Hunter standing alone in the centre circle a precursor of what was to follow. He was sacked the next day.

Former player John Breckin was made caretaker before Dave Cusack was offered the job prior to Christmas. He started well enough, with wins in his first three games, but the Millers soon slid into trouble, and after a 4-0 loss at Notts County, player-manager Cusack was sacked after 126 days in charge.

Ex-player Billy McEwan, a no-nonsense Scot, was recruited and he had the task of saving Rotherham with three games to go. He started well, with wins over Aldershot and Gillingham, but a 4-1 beating by champions Sunderland on the final day of the regular followed. As other results went against them, they dropped into the bottom four for the only time that year, and it meant they faced a relegation play-off against Swansea. The Millers lost 1-0 in the first leg at Vetch Field and drew 1-1 in the return, Johnson scoring, to drop the club into the fourth tier for the second time in its history.

But despite the doom and gloom, in McEwan Rotherham had appointed a manager with enough steel to pull the club up by its bootstraps. McEwan spent the summer prior to 1988/89 clearing the decks. Players were released and in came the likes of the experienced Billy Russell, Pat Heard and Bobby Williamson.

The response was startling. United won five of their first six League games to climb straight to the top and McEwan kept the momentum up with fifth place being the lowest the team dropped all year. They met Manchester United for the first time since that 1966 epic in the League Cup, losing 1-0 at Millmoor before a 5-0 defeat at Old Trafford in the second leg, but everyone knew that it was the League that mattered. Williamson was the key to the success, just as top strikers such as Ronnie Moore, Jack Shaw and Wally Ardron had been in years gone by. The Scot hit twenty-eight League and cup goals, proving a spectacular success for a free transfer, and it was a 3-1 win at Stockport, with an army of Millers fans travelling across the Pennines in fancy dress, which clinched promotion with a game to go. A draw at home to Cambridge on a carnival final day saw Rotherham take only their third-ever championship.

The 1989/90 season saw a solid end to an often traumatic decade. McEwan steered his side to a comfortable ninth place after a bright start that saw Cardiff clattered 4-0, Birmingham beaten 5-1, Williamson scoring hat-tricks in both, and Leyton Orient blasted 5-2 in successive games at Millmoor. In November, the goals continued to flow and a 5-0 thrashing of Chester, followed by a 4-2 victory over Shrewsbury put Rotherham second, two points off the top.

It didn't last and despite the subsequent tailing-off everyone, particularly McEwan, could be pleased with the overall picture at Millmoor.

McEwan, though, wouldn't last another season.

How Millmoor looked from the air in 1965.

Left: Manager Tom Johnson.

Below: The 1960/61 League Cup final team.

Above: Rotherham United, 1964/65.

Below: The 1966 United team.

Left: Brian Tiler, one of the star players of the sixties.

Below: Goalkeeper Alan Hill.

Above left: Tommy Docherty meets the players in November 1967.

Above right: Tommy Docherty at his desk.

Below: Tommy Docherty with skipper Brian Tiler.

Left: Tommy Docherty
at Millmoor.

Below: The 1970 Millers team.

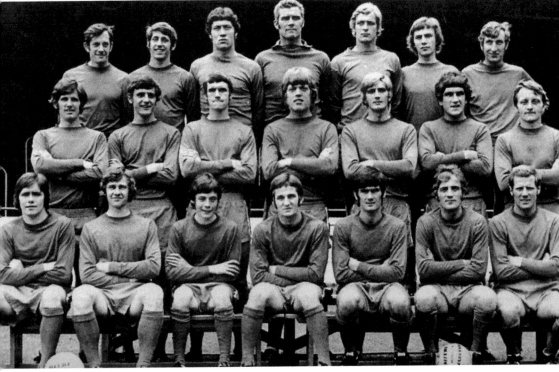

Right: Dave Watson in action in 1969.

Below left: The programme from the Millers *v.* Leeds FA Cup clash in 1970.

Below right: Ray Mielczarek.

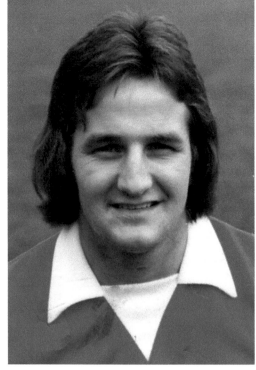

Above left: Striker Carl Gilbert.

Above right: Trevor Phillips.

Below left: Trevor Swift.

Alan Crawford in action against Brighton in 1975.

Dick Habbin goes for goal in 1975.

Above left: Midfield maestro Jimmy Goodfellow.

Above right: David Gwyther in 1976.

Below: Millmoor.

Above: Rodney Fern scores against Bristol City in 1979.

Below left: Paul Stancliffe in action.

Below right: Paul Stancliffe head shot.

Above: Defender Gerry Forrest.

Below left: Manager Ian Porterfield.

Below right: Mark Rhodes in action at Huddersfield in 1980 with Mick Gooding in support.

Above: New men ... Ronnie Moore, Tony Towner and John Seasman arrive at Millmoor in 1980.

Right: Tony Towner celebrates the Millers' winner against Sheffield United in February 1981.

Richard Finney scores the opener at Bramall Lane in 1980/81. The Millers won 2-1.

The 1980/81 title winners.

Above: John Seasman heads for goal in 1982 with Ronnie Moore in support.

Right: Emlyn Hughes receives the Manager of the Month award for February 1982.

10

A DOWNWARD SPIRAL ... BUT THE MILLERS WIN AT WEMBLEY

The highest position the Millers achieved in a difficult 1990/91 season was fifteenth, as they failed to build for the demands of a higher division. Billy McEwan was hamstrung by finance as chairman Ken Booth kept a tight grip on the purse strings. That was to be a common theme for over two decades at Millmoor.

It took four games for them to get off the mark, to a 5-1 victory over Wigan at Millmoor with lanky Stewart Evans grabbing two. But five straight defeats afterwards left fans in no doubt that they were in for a tough ride, especially when top scorer Williamson was sold to Kilmarnock for £100,000 and promising midfield product Martin Scott went to Bristol City for a club record £200,000.

Rotherham dropped to the foot of the table and then, in November, speculation began to mount that McEwan's job was under threat. The manager offered to resign as results continued to keep the club pinned at the bottom, and when United were thrashed 5-0 at Swansea on New Year's Day it proved the final straw. The board met and, in true Rotherham style, didn't tell anyone that they hadn't sacked McEwan, but rather had pushed him to one side. When the Millers travelled to Swansea again four days later in the third round of the FA Cup, McEwan was strangely absent and inquisitive reporters were told that he'd been put on gardening leave and was 'away scouting'. Assistant boss Phil Henson had picked the team that ground out a 0-0 draw and McEwan was told to stay away from Millmoor.

The situation became ridiculous. Exactly what the club was thinking was hard to fathom, and McEwan didn't deserve to be put through what was happening. Perhaps the club got their wish when McEwan resigned and Henson took over but, despite six wins in their last thirteen games, they dropped out of the division in second-bottom place.

Henson was the seventh manager inside a decade and he made an immediate impact, despite the club having debts of over half a million pounds, which restrained his transfer activities. He signed strikers Tony Cunningham and Don Page and four wins in their first six games saw them shoot up to the top of the table.

Cunningham and Page proved to be the perfect target men, netting eighteen and eleven goals respectively, and Henson astutely brought in another young goal-getter in the form of Bermudian Shaun Goater. With a solid defence, shackled together by Nicky Law, Nigel Johnson and quality playmakers such as local lads Shaun Goodwin and Dean Barrick, plus the experienced Mark Todd, United recorded nine wins in their last twelve games to finish second, six points behind runaway leaders Burnley. Promotion was clinched with a 3-0 win at Wrexham in the penultimate game.

That season was also notable for the Millers being involved in the first-ever penalty shootout in the FA Cup, when they overcame Scunthorpe in the opening round.

Back in what was then renamed Division Two, formerly the Third Division, Rotherham needed stability. Things looked bright as Henson signed a new contract, the 30-acre training ground was opened at Hooton Lodge on the outskirts of town, and they started with a 2-0 win at Exeter. By Christmas, with a string of good wins under their belt, Rotherham was up to second. In the League Cup they gave Premiership big guns Everton a scare when Goater netted in a 1-0 first-leg victory, only to lose 3-0 in a controversial second when goalkeeper Billy Mercer was red-carded.

In the FA Cup, United progressed to the third round where they met Kevin Keegan's Newcastle at Millmoor in front of a sell-out 13,000, the capacity having been drastically reduced following the Taylor Report into the Bradford City fire disaster. In the replay, Rotherham fought bravely at St James' Park but went out 2-0, unable to replicate the achievements of the famous win there four decades earlier. But in the League, Rotherham slid down the table but still finished a pleasing eleventh.

The 1993/94 season saw them again embroiled in a relegation battle, with more ups and downs than a yo-yo, but it was a 7-0 beating of Hartlepool in April, rising star Goater hitting four, that gave them the impetus to drive clear of the drop zone and finish fifteenth. The big problem heading into the next campaign was that a raft of players were out of contract, Henson reluctantly accepting a scant one-year extension to his contract, and it was only late in the day that the squad was assembled.

For the first time there was talk that the club might look to move from the increasingly unsuitable Millmoor, especially with Football Trust funding available. But despite looking at potential sites, the deadline for the grants came and went and they were be stuck at the old ground for a lot longer to come.

Things weren't going too swimmingly on or off the pitch. When United were rocked 4-0 at home by Shrewsbury on the opening day, Ken Booth was lambasted by a gathering of fans, especially when some stayed behind to protest. Booth responded by saying that he'd listen to offers, although how much he'd listed was conjecture. A gruff-talking scrap dealer, he had his own way of dealing with issues both in his workplace next to Millmoor or at the club. Sections of the crowd pilloried him for years, finding it hard to understand why he wouldn't put more money in, but they didn't see the hefty cheques that he frequently signed just to keep the club alive.

There remain complex arguments, plus the understanding that his accountant told him to hang on to the Millers for tax reasons, but despite his failings, Ken Booth kept Rotherham United alive in the 1990s – although, it has to be said, his dealings a decade later did almost kill the club off.

Henson lasted just seven disappointing League games in 1994/95 before he was surprisingly made chief executive, with long-serving secretary Norman Darnill made redundant. In a welter of publicity, John McGovern and Archie Gemmill took charge as joint managers in September and their first game was a 2-0 victory at Hull.

The Scots tried to establish their own brand of football but, just as Emlyn Hughes had found ten years earlier, it was difficult to make it work in a lower division. They were told in no uncertain terms that there was no cash. In a forgettable first year, Rotherham finished seventeenth, again chopping and changing the squad, dispensing with the likes of Mark Todd, Des Hazel and Andy Williams and bringing in winger Andy Roscoe, seasoned striker Bobby Davison and central defender Mark Monington.

McGovern and Gemmill didn't achieve what they wanted in the League at Rotherham – far from it – but 1995/96 brought a massive first for the club – their debut appearance at Wembley. While the Millers were stuttering from forgettable game to forgettable game in Division Two, a 5-1 home win over Peterborough being the highlight and a 7-0 thrashing at Wrexham the lowlight, it was the Auto Windscreens Shield that captured the imagination of the town.It is one of those competitions where people rarely remember the early rounds, but after United had disposed of Chester, Burnley, Wigan – in front of a record low 1,008 Millmoor crowd – and Lincoln, a 4-1 home win over York City suddenly made supporters realise that they were a semi-final away from a maiden trip to the Twin Towers.

They met Carlisle United over two legs and goals from Shaun Goater and Neil Richardson gave them a 2-0 win. It meant Rotherham had a big advantage going into the second leg at Brunton Park, when it was Nigel Jemson, a well-travelled striker on loan from Notts County, who was the hero with a brace in a 2-1 victory.

So the town exploded in Wembley fever, forgetting the fact that the team was too close to the bottom four for comfort, as the Millers prepared for the final against Shrewsbury Town on 14 March. Nearly 25,000 followers from Rotherham, swamping the 10,000 from Shropshire, made the trip to London for a memorable day. Jemson was again the hero, the diminutive striker netting twice in a 2-1 victory.

But on the flipside, the final position of sixteenth in the League wasn't good enough, signings such as Mike Jeffrey from Newcastle didn't work out, and 1996/97 saw McGovern and Gemmill sacked after losing five of their first seven games, plus a League Cup exit against fourth-tier Darlington.

As the Scots cleared out their office, Danny Bergara was ushered in by Ken Booth. He might not have been the best manager Rotherham United has ever had but he had the longest name – Daniel Alberto Bergara de Medina – and the Uruguayan certainly was charismatic. Top scorer with Real Mallorca as a player, he had managerial experience at Rochdale and Stockport, having also coached at Sheffield United, and after losing his first game at Gillingham he chalked up the first win of a tough season with a 1-0 victory over Burnley.

But by then Rotherham were stuck at the bottom and just one win from the next fifteen games left Bergara with eighteen measly points from twenty-five games. Relegation was confirmed with four games to go as they scored an all-time low of thirty-nine goals, with the top scorer being Earl Jean with just six.

By this time the supporters were in a flux. The *Advertiser* organised a crisis meeting at a packed club in the town centre that was attended by all of the board, minus the chairman and Bergara. If anything, it did demonstrate the depth of feeling on the terraces. For all his charm, Bergara was dismissed before the end of the season and the board realised they needed to make the right appointment with fears that, given the flimsy strength of the squad, the Millers could plunge straight through Division Three.

Bobby Williamson scores.

Derby action from the Millers 1-1 draw with Chesterfield in May 1992, which was enough to give them promotion from the old Division Four.

Wembley, 1996. The Millers' line-up before the Auto Windscreens Shield win over Shrewsbury.

Goal ... Nigel Jemson scores the Millers' second at Wembley.

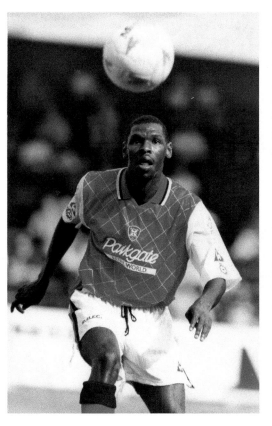

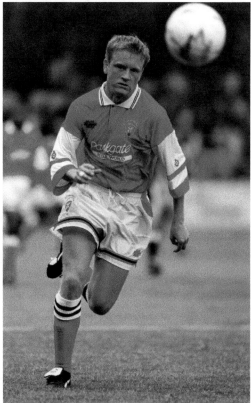

Above left: Shaun Goater.

Above right: Chris Wilder in action.

Below right: John McGovern and Archie Gemmill.

Dressing room celebrations at Hartlepool.

Goalkeeper Bobby Mimms.

11

RONNIE'S BACK ...
AND IT'S TAKE-OFF TIME

Ronnie Moore arrived at Millmoor to a welcome the like of which had never been seen before. Rotherham had had big name managers, but when the man who had been the darling of the terraces in the early eighties was brought in from Southport, the reaction was astonishing. They queued in their hundreds for a welcome home night at a Rotherham nightclub, and when he was paraded at Millmoor, the roof nearly lifted off the Tivoli End.

Moore had actually applied for the vacant Rotherham job when he was tipped off that McGovern and Gemmill were about to be axed, only for his letter to mysteriously disappear, presumably due to someone at the Millmoor End. But the *Advertiser* set the ball rolling when Bergara left and this time the maelstrom of enthusiasm led to his appointment in time for the 1997/98 campaign. It was the beginning of one of the best chapters in the club's history.

Moore had only a handful of contracted players when he took over and began a massive rebuilding job. He started with a 3-2 home defeat against Barnet and United then lost 2-1 at Cambridge. But Moore's maiden win came as Hartlepool were beaten 2-1 at Millmoor thanks to Trevor Berry and Andy Hayward, and Rotherham went on to achieve the stability they initially needed, being steered to ninth place. Goater was the top marksman with seventeen, including hitting all four in a 5-4 Christmas win over Hull.

Moore's impact, given his resources, hadn't been immediate, but the following year things did start to look good as the Millers romped to wins in their first four games. Going into November they topped the table, with newcomer Leo Fortune-West coming in and netting twelve goals in his twenty games – including a hat-trick of headers on a 3-0 win over Carlisle.

Moore gave chances to youngsters such as Paul Hurst, Chris Sedgwick and Andy Monkhouse and more seasoned heads like Paul Warne and Steve Thompson gave them the edge of experience they needed. A fifth-placed finish saw Moore make the promotion play-offs for the first time in the Millers' history, and when they drew 0-0 at Leyton Orient in the first post-season game it raised hoped that they would again be off to Wembley – only for the Londoners to come to town and defend resolutely with the match also ending goalless. Orient won the subsequent penalty shootout 4-2.

It meant another season in Division Three, but going into the new millennium, Moore's men were in no mood to make a mistake. They started with two defeats in the first three games, but with Fortune-West again scoring regularly and backed by a well-balanced side, they climbed up the table and, going into the new century, a 2-1 win over Southend put them in top spot.

Five games without a win saw them displaced by Swansea, but a 2-1 victory at Hartlepool in the penultimate game of the season (Fortune-West and defensive hard man Guy Branston) set the champagne corks popping.

What should have been the perfect conclusion to the season, a title decider at home to Swansea, who held a one-point advantage at the top, turned into a horrendous afternoon. Crowd violence, with over 10,000 in Millmoor, marred the afternoon and it ended in tragedy when a forty-two-year-old Swansea supporter died after being trampled by a police horse outside the ground. The game ended 1-1, Lee Glover netting from the sport for United, and they had to settle for second place.

Despite that finale, the Millers took their place in football's third tier, and were promptly made favourites to immediately go back down. But what transpired was one of the most incredible seasons so far in the club's history – with a breath-taking finale to boot.

Again, United started poorly, with two wins in their first six games, despite having signed former Manchester United star Mark Robins, including a 6-1 battering at Cambridge the day after Fortune-West was sold to Cardiff for £300,000. Moore moved quickly in the transfer market, signing striker Alan Lee from Burnley for £150,000, and Rotherham promptly went on a run of ten games without defeat. When Robins and Hurst netted in a 2-0 win over Port Vale just before Christmas, it put the Millers on top of the table.

One familiar thread in the club's long history is inconsistency, and it again reared its frustrating head as United went five without a win before five straight wins, against Vale, Cambridge, Wrexham, Stoke and Colchester. This put them back in second place going into March. Moore, with the trusty club stalwart John Breckin as his assistant, then won another five out of seven, to spark talk of a second successive promotion. It almost ended when they lost at bottom club Oxford and were beaten 4-0 at top side Millwall in successive away games at the start of April, but victories against Northampton, Wigan and Luton saw the Millers take on Brentford at Millmoor in the penultimate game. If results went their way, they'd be up.

The Bees were determined to be party poopers and led after just five minutes through future target Lloyd Owusu. Stewart Talbot levelled before the break and when news came through that promotion rivals Reading were losing to Colchester in the second half, it became clear that one more goal would clinch it there and then.

There were only a couple of minutes left and it seemed as though the season would go to the final week at Peterborough before, in a moment of magical Millers history, Kevin Watson threaded a ball through to lanky striker Lee. With his back to goal, he swivelled and hit the sweetest of left-footers past the Brentford 'keeper Olafur Gottskalksson. The ground erupted as never before and Rotherham United were on their way to Division One.

Said Lee afterwards, of one of the most famous goals in club history:

I received the ball on the edge of the area from Kevin Watson and had my back to goal. I don't know what made me do it but everything seemed to come off perfectly. I knew it was on target but I was falling away and couldn't really tell if it was in. Then I heard the crowd noise and I knew.

United went up in second place, five points clear of Reading.

In 2001/02, Rotherham were quickly made favourites to go straight back down. That was accentuated when they failed to win in their first ten games but Moore's side, with much the same squad as the previous year, finally got off the mark when a Robins double gave them a 2-0 win over Grimsby.

Rotherham put enough points in the bank to achieve their aim – survival – and the season was made all the more memorable when they came from 2-0 down to draw at Sheffield United and then travelled to Hillsborough, backed by 6,000 fans, in February and snatched a 2-1 win thanks to Alan Lee and local lad (and Wednesdayite) Richie Barker. The Millers finished fourth from the bottom, staving off the drop despite not winning any of their last ten games.

Into 2002/03 and Rotherham made their best-ever start to a campaign as they went to Millwall and hammered the Londoners 6-0 with striker Darren Byfield, signed for the final three games of the previous year, bagging four. That set the pulses racing and Rotherham were unbeaten in their next four games, including another win at Hillsborough. In an uncanny repeat of what had happened six months earlier, the derby game looked to be heading for a draw, until Darren Garner collected the ball 25 yards out and rifled home an injury time winner. They went on to put four past both Walsall and Stoke before swamping Burnley 6-2 thanks to doubles from Lee, Byfield and midfielder John Mullins. The rest of the campaign brought mixed fortunes but Rotherham were highly satisfied with a fifteenth-place finish.

It was more of the same in 2003/04. They beat West Ham 1-0 at Millmoor on the day the Hammers embarrassingly refused to change at the ground, saying the facilities weren't good enough, and opted to use a nearby hotel instead. After that, the Millers crashed to four heavy defeats, Moore propping up the squad by signing Martin Butler from Reading for £150,000 and then swapping Byfield for Sunderland's Michael Proctor. Butler went on to top score with fifteen as Rotherham again did enough to keep their heads above water in seventeenth place, the League programme being punctuated by a terrific League Cup performance at Arsenal when they battled to a 1-1 draw before bowing out 9-8 on penalties.

But there was always the feeling that Rotherham was on thin ice in the second tier, just as they had been in the early eighties. That came to pass in 2004/05 as they dropped out of the newly named Championship like a stone. They went twenty games without a League win at the start before Martin McIntosh's goal gave them a 1-0 win over Leeds.

It was a torrid season. Rotherham won just five times and finished fifteen points adrift at the bottom. But it was off the field where most attention was focused.

Above: Alan Lee scores the famous late goal against Brentford that earned promotion in 2001.

Left: Paul Hurst.

12

THAT OLD BLACK MAGIC

Some believe in black magic; others treat the notion with disdain. But this is a true story.

One day, in 2003, the tea bars were being stacked up and made ready for that weekend's game. During the afternoon, the stadium manager saw a person he didn't recognise inside the ground, who had been lending a helping hand to a friend with the tea bar work. The person was ejected from Millmoor, despite protestations that he'd only been helping out, which he had. Maddened, he mentioned it to a friend of his that night, who just happened to practice the dark arts. His friend came up with the idea of putting a curse on the club. A few days later they both turned up at the Millmoor forecourt, armed with potions and candles, sat cross-legged on the car park and, to the amazement of the girls in club shop and passers-by, began incanting the ritual.

Hogwash? Maybe ... but that was at the start of the season the Millers collapsed out of the Championship and were plunged into the worst financial crisis in their history.

During late 2004, the struggling club was losing money hand-over-fist and Ken Booth, prompted by his family, who had no desire to maintain an interest in football, began talks with a supporters' group, who later became known as Millers 05. When they eventually took over on 1 January 2005, the high-earning Moore was the first casualty. Results clearly were the main reason, especially a 3-0 home defeat by Yeovil in the FA Cup, but the fact that the manager was a high earner – and the priority was balancing the books – didn't help his argument.

Like several instances in the club's history, there have been major points of argument. Millers 05's ill-fated stint at the helm was initially seen as a rescue mission, but some of the decisions they made, bearing in mind the new board comprised of solid-state businessmen, were impossible to fathom. The biggest mistake they made was allowing Ken Booth to take over ownership of the ground in deference to the £3 million he was owed by Rotherham United, plus a £600,000 loan to allow the club to see the season out. It was a move they had to make, but that single decision very nearly forced the club out of existence in the most turbulent period in its history.

Moore was sacked at the end of January and, in April, Mick Harford was appointed. That summer, Millers 05 went ahead with plans to build a new main stand, seen as another move they had to make. It should have been a venture to bring in much-needed corporate revenue but, plagued by problems, it was never completed. In 2005/06 there was initial optimism as United climbed to fourth, but the slide then started and after thirteen winless games, culminating in a 2-1 home defeat against Yeovil in December, the new board sacked their second manager inside a year.

Alan Knill, Harford's assistant, took over, and by the time March came around they were into the bottom four and looked destined for the drop. But three wins in five games saw them clamber out of the drop zone and they went into the final game, at home to MK Dons, needing to avoid defeat to avoid the drop. A 0-0 draw was enough and they finished fifth from the bottom with the Dons instead going down.

But as the Millers were scrambling their way to eventual survival, things were stirring in the boardroom and Millers 05 found themselves teetering under a growing mountain of debt, with the club losing a staggering £140,000 a month. Now that they didn't own the ground, they had no tangible assets to offer as surety to the bank. The 'Save the Millers' campaign was launched to try and raise £1 million with fans from far and wide rallying to the cause. Bucket collections were held at neighbouring grounds, sponsored walks were held, Sheffield United agreed to pay the full wages of loan players Stephen Quinn and Jonathan Forte and Sheffield Wednesday bought Deon Burton for £110,000, paid up front rather than in the usual instalments.

It didn't work and, as Rotherham faced the prospect of going to the wall, a last-gasp agreement was struck with businessmen – and staunch fans – Denis Coleman and Dino Maccio. They stepped in to try and repair the damage that had been caused during the previous tenure but could do nothing to stop the club from entering a Company Voluntary Arrangement, which saw creditors take a penny in the pound but which allowed the club to continue trading. They were also docked ten points and Knill faced the thankless task of assembling a squad for 2006/07 after he was left with just seven professionals on the books.

He did piece together a squad but, saddled with the point's deduction, it was too much as Rotherham staggered from defeat to defeat and slumped to the bottom of the table. A run which saw one win in eighteen League games brought the dismissal of Knill on 1 March with assistant Mark Robins, who had done such a good job in the youth department, was handed the reins. He started with a 4-1 victory over Bradford City, Delroy, Facey and Martin Woods netting doubles, but Robins could do nothing to stop Rotherham from again being relegated with three games left, fourteen points away from safety.

For 2007/08, the wounded Millers were back in League Two. Still, fans were thankful that the club was still alive and hadn't gone the way of Scarborough and subsequently Halifax Town. But they weren't out of the woods yet.

In 2007/08, Robins gave young guns such as Will Hoskins, Marc Newsham and Stephen Brogan their chance and, after a shaky opening, seven straight wins took them up with the front-runners. They even reached second place at one stage before the inevitable downturn came, although in March they were still well placed for a play-off shot. But Coleman and Maccio were struggling, especially with having to pay a staggering weekly rent back to the Booth family on top of the regular losses. They sold Will Hoskins and Lee Williamson to Watford, but on 18 March the club again went into administration, leading to another ten-point deduction.

Coleman and Maccio meant well, but were way out of their depth when it came to the financial demands of the game and also the stranglehold put on the club by the agreement with the Booths. For all of Ken Booth's good work in keeping the club alive, it was disappointing to see him and his family sticking to their guns, demanding their payments and a 'family package' deal that saw them get the Millers' allocation of four FA Cup final tickets and even get use of the club physiotherapist. Board member Giles Brearley described the agreement, struck with Millers 05, as 'madness', especially as it was to run for eighty years! Coleman and Maccio also had to adhere to a lease agreement which, despite them not owning the ground, left them liable for any repairs, as well as having to pay a reported £15,000 a week in rent.

Entering another bout of administration led to the departure of the two businessmen and saw United's form slip. They ended up ninth, fourteen points off the play-offs after the point deduction. They were bleak times indeed, but few supporters could have envisaged what was just over the horizon.

Several people applied to the administrator, including Coleman, but Sheffield-born businessman Tony Stewart was the one who was named as prospective new owner. If ever there was a knight in shining armour, wearing a red-and-white scarf, it was him, even though he'd only been to a handful of football matches before.

The new chairman was paraded in front of the fans for the first time in the season finale, a 1-0 victory over Barnet. Young Jamie Green scored the last-ever goal at the ground.

Stewart's accession wasn't without problems. He tried to strike a deal with the Booths without any joy and once the club came out of administration, he again needed to enter a Company Voluntary Arrangement to pay off creditors. When it became clear that the Booths wouldn't yield, Stewart, who had made millions out of his ASD Lighting Empire, took the bold decision to move away from Millmoor after 101 years. He reached agreement for the club to play at Don Valley Stadium, an athletics venue in Sheffield, and was forced to pay a bond of £750,000 with an assurance that the club would be back in Rotherham in four years, plus a refund of £1 million to the Football Foundation, who had given the seven-figure grant to help build the new stand at Millmoor.

With that bridge crossed, and with the clock ticking down to the new season, the next problem was that the CVA wasn't agreed by creditors. It left a question mark over whether Rotherham would get to the start line for their August opener against Lincoln. But the League decided there were 'exceptional circumstances' at play and gave United the green light, albeit with a massive seventeen-point penalty, just three days before the big kick-off.

The new era was underway, after some of the toughest times any club has had to endure. The fact that Rotherham United was still around was testament to some rock-solid determination to stave off extinction. And then came the news that everyone wanted to hear – plans were being drawn up for a new stadium in Rotherham.

The Millers, still under Robins, began with 2008/09 with a 1-0 victory over Lincoln, with Reuben Reid, plucked from nowhere, netting the forty-fourth-minute winner in front of 4,748. That season, Rotherham would have made the play-offs but for the point deduction, which was applied at the end of the campaign. There was a bulldog spirit in the dressing room that made sure they didn't collapse under the oncoming burden, as Luton Town had in the same campaign. They lost one of their first ten games to climb up with the leaders and were in fifth spot by the time the season concluded with a 1-0 defeat at home to Exeter.

Of course, United were delighted to still be around and were happily plotting their 2009/10 campaign, including the signature of striker Adam Le Fondre from League Two rivals Rochdale, when they were hit by another bombshell.

They started well with a home win over Accrington Stanley and, despite losing at Bournemouth next time out, then won four games on the trot, culminating in a 3-1 victory over old foes Chesterfield at Don Valley, with Le Fondre, Danny Harrison and Kevin Ellison all netting in the second half to put their side top of the table. Then came the news that Robins was leaving. Rivals Barnsley had watched his progress not only that year but also under the duress of the previous year and struck a deal to take the manager and assistant John Breckin up the road to Oakwell. Tony Stewart was forced to look for a replacement and found it in the man who had catapulted Rotherham into the Championship – Ronnie Moore.

Moore was one of several candidates who applied for the position. When he was interviewed, Stewart took no notice of what had gone before and was mightily impressed by his CV, persona and ambition. After all, Stewart made no bones of the fact that he wanted big things for the club. Moore was given the job, with former player Jimmy Mullen his sidekick, and he made his second bow as United beat Barnet 3-0 at home.

Moore inherited a strong squad, Le Fondre leading the way up front, with twenty-seven goals, and a 4-2 win at Bradford in December, Ellison scoring twice, saw them sitting nicely in third place. That's where they stayed going into April, but defeats at home to Port Vale and then at Aldershot and Morecambe saw the bandwagon derailed. The Millers finished fifth, enough for them to pocket a play-off place against Aldershot.

The first game was at the Recreation Ground and it looked as though the game would end goalless until Le Fondre darted onto a bad backpass and slotted home the winner. Back at Don Valley four days later, they made no mistake as Le Fondre and Ellison wrapped up a 2-0 win.

So it was off to Wembley for a second time, on this occasion at the newly rebuilt stadium, to face Londoners Dagenham & Redbridge. But in a thrilling game, the Millers' hearts were broken as they twice came from behind thanks to local youngster Ryan Taylor only to lose to a seventieth-minute clincher.

So it was back to League Two for 2010/11, and the Millers were optimistic about another good year, with Ryan Cresswell signed as skipper and a feel-good factor beginning to emerge as Stewart unveiled plans to build a new £20-million ground on the old Guest & Chrimes steelworks side adjacent to the town centre.

United opened with a 2-1 win at Lincoln as they won three of their first four games including a 6-4 thriller against Cheltenham, with Le Fondre bagging four. By the time the New Year came around, Rotherham were up to second and hard on the heels of top dogs Chesterfield, and they continued to flirt with the top three. But progress slowed, they slipped downtable and a spell of just four wins in fourteen games proved frustrating for Stewart.

The crunch came when Rotherham went to Chesterfield on 18 March in a televised derby. They needed to win but were ripped to shreds by the Spireites and lost 5-0. Reports that Stewart left the ground early were wrong – he'd nipped outside for a cigar – but when Moore went on live television afterwards and declared that he'd shoot the lot of his players that proved too much for the chairman. Moore and Mullen were sacked with the team sixth and five points off an automatic promotion place!

The big question is whether United would have prospered further that year had Stewart, who admits he was still learning the game at that time, stuck with Moore. Certainly, the chairman felt a change was needed while Moore's subsequent exploits with Tranmere add fuel to the counter argument.

Player-coach Andy Liddell took over as caretaker and Rotherham promptly faded away to finish a disappointing ninth, by which time Stewart had appointed former Brentford boss Andy Scott. The dour Scott's arrival on a three-year contract was heralded as a good appointment – although there were some doubts emanating from West London – and there was plenty of optimism heading into 2011/12.

Scott's side carded four wins and a draw in the first five games, taking the club to the top of the table and earning him the Manager of the Month award for August. That's often the kiss of death, and so it proved as he won one game in September and things quickly started to fall apart as they plunged down to fourteenth place and only scraped home 2-1 in an FA Cup tie at Barrow.

Scott was a difficult man for many people to work with. His PR acumen was found wanting and the element of 'professionalism' he brought to the club irked such as the hardy supporters who had turned up to watch training each day, only for the new boss to have the gates closed in their faces.

On the field, results weren't good enough. The Millers slipped to mid-table, despite Scott having a hefty budget by League Two standards, and when the team lost 2-1 at Oxford in March he was sacked after less than a year in charge. His assistant, Darren Paterson, took temporary charge and he started with a 4-2 win over Maccesfield at Don Valley. Paterson hauled United back into the top ten but the damage had been done and the season fizzled out in eleventh place.

Touchline celebrations
after the final whistle
against Brentford.

Goal ... Darren garner scores the 30-yard thunderbolt to earn a 2-1 win at Hillsborough in 2002.

Goal ... Martin McIntosh gives the Millers a 1-0 win over Leeds in the Championship in 2004 – their first win of the campaign – at the twenty-first attempt.

Right: Ronnie Moore celebrates the 2-1 victory at Sheffield Wednesday in 2002.

Below: Troubled times ... fans at the centre of the Save Our Millers campaign.

Above left: Manager Alan Knill.

Below left: Ken Booth.

Below right: John Mullin celebrates staying up on the last day of the 2005/06 season.

Jamie Green scores the last-ever goal at Millmoor as the Millers beat Barnet in May 2008.

Coming down ... the old main stand is demolished.

Above left: Millmoor closes its doors after 101 years.

Above right: Manager Mark Robins.

Below: Don Valley Stadium.

13

RISING FROM THE ASHES

By the time Tony Stewart was pondering his third managerial appointment, the New York Stadium was rising majestically. Construction for the plush 12,000-capacity arena, named after the old New York area of town, had begun in February 2010 and was scheduled to be ready for the start of the 2012/13 campaign.

When the managerial decision was made, it came like a bolt out of the blue. Steve Evans, who had come through several scrapes in the past to take Crawley Town into the Football League, was named in a blaze of publicity on 9 April 2012. Evans had been involved in financial mis-dealings at Boston United and, during his last few months with Crawley, was involved in a flare-up during a match at Valley Parade for which he was, after taking over at Rotherham, subsequently banned for six games.

Evans' arrival was hardly greeted with euphoria but, regardless, Stewart saw the forty-nine-year-old as the man to lead the side into the club's new era. Evans himself, a bubbly, likeable character, had been won over by the chairman's ambition and a playing budget that was the best in the division.

The final game at Don Valley was on 5 May. Alex Revell scored in a 1-1 draw with Northampton and it was then that attention switched to one of the most momentous days in the club's history. United, with a string of new players, including former Barnsley men Daniel Nardiello and Kayode Odejayi and Icelandic international midfielder Kari Arnason, tempted to League Two from SPL giants Aberdeen, played their first game at the New York when they beat Barnsley 2-1 in a friendly on 21 July.

The 2012/13 season was a real roller-coaster ride, as Tony Stewart's gamble in pumping a fortune into the magnificent New York Stadium and giving Steve Evans the manager's job eventually paid off.

The season kicked off well, but didn't all go to plan. Evans had inherited a squad that finished seventeen points shy of automatic promotion the previous year and he had to conduct major surgery. More than thirty players came and went, and a few nips and tucks had to be performed as the weeks turned to months. Including loanees, nearly forty players were used throughout the campaign, but slowly and surely, amidst the highs – the early season destruction of Burton and Bradford – and the lows – being hit for six at Bradford and five at Dagenham – a group of players emerged that lasted the course and got it together when it mattered.

Rotherham were attack-minded, often attacking as keenly away from home as they did at the New York Stadium. That might partly explain their relatively high number of defeats, a higher number than all but one of the top seven, but also the whopping twenty-four victories, the highest in the division.

The Millers had to overcome a six-match stadium ban for the manager, after a highly publicised flare-up at Bradford City while boss at Crawley, and Evans was forced to defend his methods after a particularly awful day against Bristol Rovers at the end of January. A section of fans wanted his head on a stick, but his response was to get his head down, carry on with business and ride out the storm.

In the end, quality told. Players such as Icelandic international Kari Arnason, Craig Morgan, Lee Frecklington and Michael O'Connor brought dynamism to the side, and even though there were times, particularly towards the end of the season, when automatic promotion looked to be drifting away, there was nevertheless a feeling that the Millers had too much quality not to succeed.

They did it in style. Defeats at Gillingham and Morecambe at the beginning of April left them on the fringes, but five successive wins propelled them into League One. Exeter, with one of the best away records in the division, were thumped 4-1, and Rotherham followed that up with a 2-1 home victory over Fleetwood. The bandwagon rolled into Bradford and City were convincingly beaten 2-0 – a result that really did send hopes soaring.

The feel-good factor continued with a 1-0 win at Plymouth on the penultimate weekend and that meant United only needed to beat relegated Aldershot Town – managed by Andy Scott – on the final day to secure promotion back to the third tier.

The sell-out crowd saw skipper Johnny Mullins strike first and then Lee Frecklington wrap up a 2-0 win, which saw emotions explode.

The colourful Evans summed up the season: 'This club has been through a heck of a lot but all the hard work finally paid off – the fans deserve it after all they've been through.'

Quite. Rotherham United's history has been pretty traumatic and turbulent, summed up by the previous six years. Forget all the padlocks and witchcraft and points deductions. When those champagne corks popped after promotion was secured, believe me, they popped like never before.

The press conference to unveil Steve Evans as boss.

Pastures new ... Tony Stewart at the New York Stadium.

Celebrations at Valley Parade.

Fans invade the pitch.

Steve Evans, jumping for joy.

Steve Evans celebrates.